I'D DO IT ALL OVER AGAIN

MY STORY

By
George B. Creed

To Nathaniel (Buddy) White
We were best friends though
school. Graduation and life choices
seppparated us. When we do get together
it seems as if time melts and our
bond is as strong as ever.
I treasure our friendship
George

I'd Do It All Over Again: My Story

By George B. Creed

ISBN- 13: 978-1508952947 ISBN-10: 1508952949

Published by Creekside Publishing Company, PO Box 1848, Lincolnton NC 28093 www.cspubco.com

For additional copies of this book or to arrange a speaking engagement with the author contact:

George B. Creed, gbcreed45@gmail.com

CREDITS

The first story in this book has been handed down in my family for many years. A version of this story first appeared in print in my second cousin's book, "A Palette, Not A Portrait", stories from the life of Nathan Garrett.

His book was published in 2010. His father and the son of Julian told the story that appears in his book.

My grandmother, Geneva Williams, the firstborn daughter of Nathan Williams, told me the version of the story that is in my book.

The stories differ slightly but are presented the way they were told.

A very close friend and colleague, Dr. Marc Schoenfield has recently started composing beautiful music. The music is from his heart and details his life events. Marc is a gifted veterinarian, musician, singer and composer. Many of the songs he writes are inspired by the love he has for his wonderful wife, Anna Marie.

Long after Marc has departed this life and those of us who knew him have faded, his music will still be present. His music will stand as a testament to his life.

Inspired by this daring adventure in Marc's life and wanting a legacy of my own I decided to write this book.

I am proud to call Marc my friend but he is more like my brother.

I thank my wife of 47 years, Natalie for putting up with me and checking this book for misspellings and grammar. If you find errors, they are mine and certainly not hers. I never could spell and may have overlooked some of her corrections.

Many of the stories in this book are about my clients. Their names have been changed to protect their identities. I greatly appreciate the trust and devotion I received from all of my clients.

I pray that none of those who recognize themselves in these writings will be offended by anything I've written. It was a privilege to serve as your veterinarian for 35 years and I am truly grateful for the opportunity you afforded me

PROLOGUE

I believe everyone has a book in them. We just need the stimulus to start writing. My stimulus came from church. I was raised a Baptist. When I married Natalie, she told me we were now Methodist.

When we moved to Gastonia she looked for a local AME church. Finding none, she chose St Stephens AME Zion Church.

There's not much difference between AME and AME Zion Churches. The AME (African Methodist Episcopal) church was founded in 1787 in Philadelphia. The AME Zion church was also founded in 1787 but in New York. Both were created because segregation extended to the church even in the North. People of color were not allowed to sit in the same area as whites, vote or hold office in the church.

Today's AME Zion churches have a pastor presiding over each church. An Elder presides over a district (our district was called the Lincolnton District). A Bishop presides over several districts and the Senior Bishop presides over everything.

Rev. Stellie Jackson was our Elder. He established a monthly newsletter to inform members of upcoming events, awards and honors through out our district. Elder Jackson asked me to write a monthly article on pet health for our newsletter.

I told him, "People will be bored stiff reading about that sort of thing. Lots of amusing things have happened to me while working with animals. Why don't I write a few articles about my experiences and invite our readers to send me their own amusing stories. I will pick the best ones and send them to our publisher each month".

Elder Jackson, liked this idea. I began writing articles and for three years, no one sent me an article. The articles I wrote became a favorite part of the newsletter and were often read before any other article.

When I eventually stopped writing for the newsletter, I had the basis for a book. I kept the articles and promised myself, one day I would write a book.

That's how I got started. I hope you will enjoy my stories.

PART ONE
IN THE BEGINNING

The Williams Family

One warm Saturday evening, two hours past sunset in 1895, Nathan Williams sat on the large covered front porch of his beautiful, spacious, ranch styled home in Tarboro NC. With him were his three adult sons, Nathan Jr., Julian and Charlie. The boys were attentive but calm. Such was the nature of their father. The four were armed with pistols in hand and an arsenal of rifles, shot guns and two machine guns at their feet. The Williams women were at an aunt's house several blocks away, safe from the trouble that was sure to come that evening.

Nathan Williams was born a slave in 1843 in Tarboro, NC. His mother was a mulatto slave and cook for her master, Mr. Johnston. Their master was married with children. He was also Nathan's father. Nathan and his mother lived in the Johnston home. Mr. Johnston cared deeply for Nathan and allowed him most of the privileges given to his own children.

Mr. Johnston didn't own a plantation or a farm. He owned City Barber Shop on Main Street in downtown Tarboro. White men owned all barber shops in Tarboro but all of the barbers were colored. Tarboro had three types of barber shops; one catered to wealthy white men, one catered to working class white men and the third catered to the colored. City Barber Shop catered to wealthy white men. In Nathan's early youth, he worked as a shoeshine boy and errand boy for the customers of City Barber Shop. When Nathan was school age, Mr. Johnston removed his children from the public school system and hired a tutor to teach his children in the privacy of his home. This was done so Nathan could learn to read and write. During those days, it was against the law to teach a slave to read and write.

Nathan and his mother enjoyed a pampered life in the Johnston house. When Nathan was eight years old, his father gave him and his mother their freedom. This was twelve years before President Abraham Lincoln signed the "Emancipation Proclamation" and fourteen years before the end of the Civil War. After they were granted their freedom, Nathan's mother continued to cook for the Johnston family and Nathan continued to shine shoes at City Baber Shop. When Nathan was in his teenage years, he was taught the art of barbering and soon became the barber of choice to Tarboro's elite clientele.

When Nathan was in his early twenties, Mr. Johnston died. He shocked the Tarboro community by willing City Barber Shop to Nathan. It was unheard of for a colored man to own property, let alone such a prosperous business. Nathan was young, handsome and educated. Now, overnight, Nathan had become the wealthiest man of color in Tarboro. He was a real catch for Tarboro's young women of color. He courted and married a local woman named Mary Anderson. Nathan's complexion was very light. His mother was mulatto (one white and one colored parent) and his father was white. His hair was closer to the consistency of a white man's hair rather than a colored's. The Anderson women were fine boned and very pretty. If you didn't know the family's history, you would have sworn they were white. Tragically, Mary and their first child died during the delivery. Struck with the beauty of the Anderson women and after a suitable time of mourning,

Nathan married Mary's sister Maria (pronounced Mariah). They bought a large, brick, two-storied house on Granville Street in Tarboro and started their family.

The Williams' family home on Granville St. Tarboro, NC.

(The Williams Family: Back row- Charlie, Julian, Nathan Jr. Front row: Sarah, Maria, Julia, Geneva Nathan Sr.)

Maria blessed him with three sons followed by three daughters (Geneva, the first born daughter, was my grandmother). Again, tragedy struck the Williams family. A few years after the birth of her last child, Julia, Maria died. Nathan was devastated. He loved Maria. She had been a wonderful wife to him and a wonderful mother to their children. Nathan knew he could not run his business and care for six children without a woman's help. The stigma of a "live - in nanny" with a single man was scandalous. Nathan courted and married for the third time. This time he married Georgia Mathewson , a girl from a prominent colored family in Tarboro.

Georgia's grandfather, George Mathewson, was white and a master carpenter. His work can still be seen throughout Tarboro today. His signature trademark was "elaborate scrolled trimmings" on porches, roofs, overhangs and anywhere he could tastefully place them. George Mathewson was a man who lived well and did whatever he pleased. He never cared what people thought of him. He had plenty of money but preferred to socialize with the working class people. He never sought to become a part of Tarboro's "high society".

George Mathewson had two families. One was with his white wife who gave him three children. The other was with a colored mistress who gave him five children. He was able to provide for both wives and all eight children because of the great demand for his elaborate carpentry skills. George Mathewson built houses for all of his colored children in the colored part of town. His oldest son from his colored mistress was named George Mathewson Jr. He looked white and objected to living in the colored section of town. To pacify this son, George Sr. built George Jr. a house on Church Street on the "Mason Dixie Line" (the artificial line that divided the white neighborhood of Tarboro from the colored neighborhood).

Georgia Mathewson, the daughter of George Mathewson Jr., inherited the house when her father died. The house was an impressive place for its day. It had three bedrooms, a formal living room, a den, a formal dining room, a huge kitchen with a large pantry, a dining area, a screened room off the kitchen and an indoor bathroom. The house was wood structured, painted white ,and was sort of an inverted "L" in shape. It had a large front porch with lots of scroll workmanship. A white picket fence surrounded the front yard and half of both sides of the property. Instead of grass, white sand was used for the front and side yards. There was a cement fishpond in the front yard that had a fountain (as I write this book, the fountain still works and the pond has never needed repair). The walkway in front of the home was slanted toward the street to prevent water from accumulating in the yard. The house had a cistern (which had something to do with indoor plumbing during that time). It is my understanding that this was the first house in Tarboro to have indoor plumbing. It was one of the best-built houses in Tarboro. Nathan and Georgia now had two homes to maintain. This proved difficult so they sold the house on Granville Street and moved the family to the home on Church Street.

Georgia Mathewson home on Church Street in Tarboro, NC

Nathan trained all of his sons to be barbers. When the boys reached adulthood, Nathan Jr. and Charlie moved to Plattsburg, New York. Nathan Jr. became a barber in an upscale barber shop. Charlie studied to become a minister. Julian remained in Tarboro and worked with his father at City Barber Shop.

Things were going well for the Williams family until one Saturday morning, a week before the beginning of this story. Tarboro's mayor and police chief visited Nathan in his barber shop and asked to speak to him in private. Nathan led them to his office in a back room of the barber shop. He was told that a few individuals of Tarboro's white community were stirring up trouble. They were upset that a colored man owned a business and was living better than most of the white men in Tarboro. A Ku Klux Klan rally was planned for the coming Saturday night in a vacant field north of town. The prosperity of the Williams family was the topic of discussion. The mayor and police chief were there as friends of the family and wanted Nathan to be aware of the coming trouble.

On the way home from the barber shop, Nathan discussed this matter with Julian. They agreed to keep this to themselves so as not to alarm the women in the family. Later that evening, Julian came up with a plan. Julian's skin color was white. He decided he would don a white sheet, cover his head with a pillowcase with eyeholes, and attend the Klan Rally to learn of their plans. He borrowed a neighbor's car so his wouldn't be recognized. Julian drove to the vacant field and blended in perfectly with the Klan members. His presence was never questioned.

Julian learned that only a few disgruntled men wanted to do harm to the Williams family. Most of the Klan members were against any kind of action against the family. Nathan was prosperous but knew his place. He was a good businessman and was respectful to all people. He never flaunted his wealth and should be left alone.

The handful of disgruntled members was not going to be denied. They said some of the coloreds were beginning to think the Williams family was as good as white people. If they didn't do something about it, they might start thinking they were as good as white people too. If the Klan didn't have the guts to do anything about this family, they would do it themselves.

The leaders of the Klan asked to hear what the group intended to do. They wanted to burn down City Barber Shop. This was not an option. City Barber Shop was one of five connected businesses that consumed an entire block on Main Street. One of the businesses was a four-story hotel. It would be difficult to burn the barber shop without placing the other businesses in danger. After much discussion, it was decided the Williams' home would be burnt. Those that wanted to participate would meet in this field the following Saturday at sundown. They would wear their sheets and pillowcases and go to the Williams' home from the field.

Julian took a rambling way back to his neighbor's house to return the borrowed car and then carefully made his way back to the family home. He told his father what he had learned. Nathan Sr. immediately sent for his two sons in NY asking for their help to defend the family home. In those days, NY barber shops were also fronts for "numbers rackets" and "bookie businesses" run by city gangsters. Nathan Jr. was the barber of choice for a small time gangster in Plattsburg. Nathan Jr. asked the gangster if he would help his family. The gangster wouldn't send men that far away, but would give him all the guns and ammunition he could carry. Nathan Jr. and Charlie left NY heading to Tarboro with a car full of pistols, rifles, shotguns and two machine guns.

Saturday evening had arrived. The Williams men were sitting on the front porch attentively waiting for the arrival of the Ku Klux Klan. Eventually they heard a group of men talking in the distance. They had parked their two trucks out of sight of the Williams' home and were now advancing on foot. The Williams' men were fully alert as the sounds of men approaching increased. A small portion of the Klan, 12 in number, arrived in their hooded attire. Some of them carried clubs and unlit torches. There may have even been a handgun or two in the group. They thought their arrival at the Williams' home would be unexpected. They didn't expect resistance. They also thought the Williams family would run into their home and barricade themselves in at the sight of the Klan. Their plan was to throw lit torches through the front windows of the Williams' house. They were sure the Williams family would run out the back door and hide in the colored neighborhood as their home and all of their possessions burned. They were in no way prepared for any form of resistance and were certainly unaware of the arsenal the Williams family had procured.

The Klan was surprised when they saw the Williams men on the porch. They were confused when the men didn't retreat into the house at the sight of the Ku Klux Klan.

Nathan Sr. stood up keeping his pistol behind his back and addressed the Klan, "We don't want any trouble with the Ku Klux Klan. We haven't done anything wrong. I'm asking you kindly to leave us alone. Turn around and go back home".

The mob just stood their confused by this "nigger" addressing them and daring to give them an order to leave.

Nathan further warned, "If anyone lights a torch or raises a weapon, we will be forced to defend our home". At that point, Nathan brought the pistol from behind his back and crossed his arms making sure the pistol was not pointed at the Klansmen. At that same moment, the Williams boys stood up, crossed their arms with pistols pointed away from the Klan.

After a moment of indecision, one of the hooded Klansmen defiantly struck a match to light his torch. Julian shot him in the chest. The Klansman dropped to the ground with his unlit torch.

Nathan hollered to his sons, "Hold your fire! Hold your fire! Don't shoot! Don't shoot!" The boys did as they were told but now all three had guns pointed at the men of the Ku Klux Klan.

Everything came to a stand still. For a few seconds nobody moved. When the Klansmen realized they weren't going to be fired on, they rushed to their wounded comrade.

He was gathered up by his companions and was half carried, half dragged away as his fellow Klansmen threatened, "This ain't over. You done it now boy. We'll be back. You can count on that. We'll be back"!

The confrontation was over for the moment. The situation had escalated to a level no one had anticipated.

The Williams men stayed on guard deep into the night. They knew the Klan would return. This time they would be better prepared, better armed and bring a lot more men. A colored man had shot a white man. Some or all of the Williams family would pay dearly for this act. The one advantage the family held was that no one knew the firepower the family possessed.

Early the next morning, the sheriff, the mayor and one of the most respected pastors in Tarboro came to the Williams' home. They called out to Nathan and he met them at the gate of the picket fence surrounding the house.

The sheriff told Nathan Sr. that the man that had been shot was the deputy sheriff and that he had died during the night. The Klan wanted revenge. They knew Julian had fired the shot and wanted him turned over to the Klan or they would come after him and retaliate against the entire family.

The sheriff, the mayor and the pastor knew Nathan would never turn his son over and would fight back if the Klan tried to take him by force. They told the Klan that some of them would most likely be killed if an altercation ensued. Eventually, they convinced the Klan that more deaths weren't the answer. This situation could get way out of hand if cooler heads didn't prevail.

The Klan eventually compromised. If Julian would leave Tarboro before dawn and never return, the Williams family would be left in peace. This was a far greater solution than the Williams family had anticipated. Julian was quick to accept these terms. The deputy sheriff's family or maverick Klansmen would eventually kill him if he remained in Tarboro. Plus , his leaving would ensure the safety of the rest of his family. He hastily packed some belongings, got in his car, was escorted by the sheriff to the north side of the county line and never returned to Tarboro or any part of North Carolina.

PART TWO

My Early Years

On September 5th 1945, I was born in Tarboro, in my great grandfather's home on Church Street. I was born in the home because people of color were not allowed in Tarboro's only hospital. I was the second son of Leon Vincent Creed (an officer in the Army Air Corp and a Tuskegee Airman) and Maria Williams Burke, "Popsie".

Dad was from Key Port, New Jersey and grew up as the third child of George and Hilda Creed in a family of nine children (four boys and five girls). When dad finished high school, he spent the summer working on the New Jersey docks with several other local boys. These boys were excited because when summer ended ,they were going to attend North Carolina College for the Colored in Durham, NC.

They talked about college so much Dad decided he would go with them. He had not applied to college. He just showed up and was allowed to enroll. Things were simpler in those days. Dad had received an excellent education in New Jersey so he had no trouble with the course work in college. He tried out for the basketball team and became a star with the nickname "Hoss Creed".

Maria, "Popsie" ,was an only child of Geneva (the oldest daughter of Nathan Williams) and Joe Burke. She was raised by her mother who was a librarian in Tarboro, NC. Geneva taught school for the early part of her life and then drove the "Book Mobile" (a large van that carried books out to the country. It allowed kids and adults who couldn't come to town to have access to library books).

Popsie's father, Joe Burke, never lived with Geneva (if he did, it was for a very brief period). Popsie's birth certificate shows Geneva Burke living in Tarboro and Joe Burke living in Virginia. The responsibility of raising Popsie was left completely to Geneva.

Geneva wanted the best for her daughter and was determined to see that she pursued a college degree. After finishing her early schooling in Tarboro, Geneva sent Popsie to Durham to live with Julia (Geneva's youngest sister) and to attend North Carolina College for Colored.

My father and mother met while attending college. Dad had a light brown complexion and straight black hair. Mom was almost white with straight dark brown hair. Dad was popular with the campus women and Mom was one of the many on campus who was attracted to him.

One-day, mom's father came to visit her. Joe Burke was a big man with a very light complexion. He owned a nightclub and hotel in Virginia and traveled with a bodyguard. He always had a large cigar in his mouth. He arrived on campus in a chauffeur- driven Deisenberg (a very expensive hand built car that not many people of any color could afford). This caught my father's eye and he became very interested in the daughter of this flamboyant man. Dad and Mom began dating.

In Dad's sophomore year, President Roosevelt signed a bill to allow men of color to fight in Word War II. During this same time, the Army Air Corps experimented with a group of colored men to see if they were smart enough and capable of flying airplanes (This was a joke because colored men from the US had gone to France where they were trained and served as fighter pilots). The Tuskegee Airmen was formed at Tuskegee Institute, Alabama.

Dad wanted to be a fighter pilot. He wrote a letter to Roosevelt telling him, "I'm a colored man of better than average intelligence and I want to fight for my country. If you will allow me to train with the men of Tuskegee, I promise to remain in the Air Corp for 30 years and to make the grade of Colonel before I retire".

Dad's draft notice from the Army and his acceptance to the Army Air Corp arrived the same day.

Dad married my mother and they headed to Tuskegee. The marriage had to be kept secret because air corpsmen were not allowed to be married. Mom stayed hidden away in a private home, while dad lived and trained in the barracks of Tuskegee.

When the training period was over, Dad was not allowed to pilot a plane. He had a stigmatism in one of his eyes that required him to wear glasses. Pilots had to have 20/20 vision. Dad became a navigator and bombardier.

The Air Corp moved him around quite a bit. Sometimes Mom could follow and other times it wasn't possible. On those occasions, Mom lived with her Aunt Julia in Durham and other times with her mother in Tarboro. My older brother Leon was born in Durham and I was born in Tarboro.

My earliest memories are more like flashes of incidents. I can remember white, wooden, two storied barracks arranged in rows. My mother said this was an air base in Columbus Ohio. A white girl my age with bright red hair lived there and we played together. She had a long haired Dachshund dog named "Red Wing". My mother said, "You would remember the dog's name".

Another flash memory was of my standing beside my great aunt Julia's cement fishpond holding two dead snakes on a stick. The strange thing is that in my memory, one of the snakes was pink and the other blue. There are no known snakes of either color. Maybe this memory was really a dream but we aren't supposed to dream in color, are we?

My mother did her best to keep the family together. When Leon and I reached school age, my mother decided she wanted her children to have a stable school environment. She stopped following my father and stayed with my great aunt Julia in Durham, NC. That decision would eventually cost her the marriage.

When I was about seven, my mother and father bought a house at 1306 Rosewood St. in Durham, NC. It was a small house in the colored neighborhood. It had two bedrooms, one bathroom, a kitchen, dining room and a living room. Mom lived in that house for 45 years and it was there, in the master bedroom where she drew her last breath. Mom took a secretarial job at NCC and worked at the college in various positions all of her working life.

1306 Rosewood St

Life was great. The neighborhood was full of kids our own age. We were on the outer edge of Durham City limits. The land beyond our neighborhood was wooded and undeveloped. The city bought some of the wooded area and built a low cost housing development called McDougal Terrace. We called it "The Projects". The housing units were apartments with a various numbers of bedrooms. Most were narrow with two stories. There were usually four or five apartments to a building. The Projects were built in three stages and eventually housed more than five hundred families.

This greatly increased our number of playmates. Some of the "Project Kids" didn't like the kids on my street because our families owned homes.

McDougal Terrace

I spent a lot of time in the woods catching various critters. My mother refused to wash my pants unless the pockets were turned inside out. She had run into one or two of my critters while doing the laundry. I had a love for animals at a very young age and wanted to be a veterinarian from the time I was six years old.

Colored Water

My childhood was spent in segregated times. Durham was divided racially by a railroad track which separated the white community from the colored community. We had most of what we needed in our own community so we seldom had to go across the railroad tracks.

We were not allowed to go into the white part of town alone. If possible, an adult accompanied us. If this was not possible we were to go in a group of three or four. This was large enough to offer a measure of protection but not so large as to be mistaken for a gang.

One day, I went to downtown Durham with three of my friends. We walked to town but decided to ride the bus home. We were waiting outside of a five and dime store called Kress when one of our group needed to use the bathroom. We were taught to always stay together so all of us went into Kress together. Three of us waited outside of the bathroom while the one that needed to go went in to the rest room marked "colored".

While we waited, I wanted a drink of water. There were two fountains plainly marked. One said "colored" and the other said "white". I wanted to try the water from the white fountain. My friends were nervous. We could get in a lot of trouble if caught doing something like that.

I talked them into standing in front of the fountain to block the vision of anyone who might pass by.

I got behind my friends and took a long sip from the fountain marked "white".

When I finished, they asked, "Well! How did it taste?"

I answered, "Good!"

They said, "Better than colored water?"

I answered, "Much better."

The water wasn't better. It came from the same pipe, divided to send one pipe to the white fountain and the other to the colored. I had been conditioned to think everything for white people was better than the same things meant for colored people. In my mind the water tasted better.

One by one, my friends snuck behind the barrier of comrades to taste the forbidden water. We all agreed. White water tasted better than colored water.

When I got home, I ran to my bedroom. My brother was lying across his bed studying a school assignment.

I yelled, "Guess what Leon!"

Without looking up and somewhat aggravated by this intrusion on his quiet moment, he said, "What!"

I said, "A bunch of us went downtown and tasted the water from the white fountain".

He said, "So."

Not deterred by his lack of interest I continued, "It taste better than colored water."

"Without looking up and without showing any real interest he said, "That's stupid. It's all the same water."

I said, "No! We all tasted it and agree, white water taste better!"

He just ignored me at this point. He wasn't going to argue or listen to anything I had to say on the matter. I was determine to prove to him that white water taste better than colored water.

I bade my time and eventually had a chance to go back downtown. I was with my aunt. I wore a jacket even though it was summertime and quite hot. Hidden in the inside pocket of my coat was a small glass jar with a lid.

When my aunt had finished her shopping and we were waiting for the bus in front of the Kress store, I told my aunt, "I need a drink of water."

She said, "Wait until you get home."

Perplexed, I answered, "I'm thirsty now."

She answered, "You'll never be that thirsty."

I didn't understand that comment. It was years later before I finally understood what she was trying to teach me. My complexion was light enough that if someone observed me drinking from the white fountain, it wouldn't be questioned. People would assume I was white. My aunt was lighter than me and could easily pass for white. She was an intelligent woman, had married an intelligent man and had many intelligent children. She was not going to allow anyone to define her as inferior just because of her race.

But I digress. I wanted to get water from the white fountain. So I tried again, "I need to go to the bathroom, real bad."

She looked at me really hard for a minute. I was jumping up and down and holding myself. She relented and said, "Well, go ahead but hurry back. I don't want to miss this bus".

I rushed into Kress. I went straight to the fountain. I pulled out my jar, unscrewed the lid and boldly filled my jar not caring who saw me. I put the jar back into my inside pocket and smiled all of the way home.

When I reached my aunt's house, I immediately sought my brother. I found him on the side porch. I boldly pulled out my jar and held it up for him to see,

He said, "What's that""?

I smiled and said, "White water. Taste it."

He looked at me for a moment, took the jar from my hand, unscrewed the lid, and tasted the water. He said, "Its just plain old water."

I couldn't believe it. I snatched the jar from him and took a big gulp.

He was right. It was just plain old water. I was convinced that the water my friends and I had tasted weeks earlier tasted better than colored water.

There was only one logical conclusion. If you take white water back into the colored section of town, it turns into colored water.

Love Of Animals

My great aunt Julia recognized my love of animals, because she also had a love of animals. She was the one who suggested that when I grew up, I should be a veterinarian and she would be my nurse. I didn't know what a veterinarian was.

One day she took me with her to see Dr. Vines, her German Shepherd's veterinarian. Dr. Vines was white (as were all veterinarians in NC and in most of the country in those days) and had a well-established practice in the affluent area of Durham, NC.

When my aunt told him of my love for animals, he carried us on a tour of his facility. It was magnificent. It was spotlessly clean. The surgery area was as impressive as any human hospital. The professionalism of Dr. Vines and his staff was remarkable even by today's standards. I was hooked. I wanted to be a veterinarian from that day forward. I was six years old.

The first Christmas after Mom and Dad had acquired a home in Durham, mom gave me a tiny black Cocker Spaniel puppy as a gift. I named him "George's Wee Wiggles". I loved that little dog and kept him constantly at my side. We didn't have the money or means to carry the pup for vaccinations and before long, the pup was sick. We had one of mom's girlfriends carry us to a local veterinarian. He diagnosed Wiggles with distemper. He explained that even with treatment (which we couldn't afford), the dog may not survive. If he survived, he would probably have permanent neurological damage. He advised us that the kindest thing to do would be to "put him to sleep". I kissed Wee Wiggles goodbye and cried all the way home. I vowed that one day I would become a veterinarian and I would be free. When I did become a veterinarian, I ,of course couldn't be free however, I kept my prices low enough that almost anyone could afford them.

Over the years, I visited Dr. Vines Hospital many times. Sometimes with my aunt and other times with my own animals. Dr. Vines always knew me by name and asked if I still intended to be a veterinarian. Years later when I had graduated from Veterinary School and was living in Durham, I went to his office to thank him for starting me on the path of veterinary medicine. During our talk, I told him how impressed I was that he remembered my name and ambition though years had passed between my visits. Dr. Vines had an embarrassed look on his face and said, "I'm going to let you in on one of my trade secrets." He had his secretary bring in one of his clients' files. Stapled to the inside of the file was some personal information that he collected on this client's first visit. It had the name and age of her children, information about her husband's line of work, and his name. Each file was different. When a client checked in that day, Dr. Vines reviewed the clients record to study the patient's history and also to remind him of who the client was. He would always ask about her children by name and inquire about her husband. This personal knowledge endeared him to his clients. I used this technique some when I started my practice. I later gave it up because I developed personal relationships with most of my clients and didn't need reminders to know who they were.

The Worse Christmas In My Life

I was eight years old. Mom told me that my father would be home for Christmas. I was really excited. Dad always sent elaborate gifts but I don't remember him ever being home during Christmas. I thought this would be the best Christmas ever.

Dad arrived and everyone was very happy. Mom even asked my older brother Leon and me if we wanted a little sister. We said, "NO!" Christmas Eve, Leon and I were sitting under the Christmas tree shaking presents and trying to guess what was in them. Mom was cooking breakfast and told us to go wake up Dad. We both rushed down the hall and into the master bedroom. We burst into the bedroom hollering, "Dad".

Dad was awake, sitting on the edge of the bed looking at a picture from his wallet. He told us to come and sit on either side of him. He showed us the picture he was studying. The picture was of a young Japanese woman. He asked which would we rather have for a mother, the Japanese woman or our Mom. Of course we said Mom.

I jumped off the bed and ran into the kitchen hollering to Mom, "Mom! Dad showed us a picture of some woman and asked us which we would rather have for a mother, her or you. We both said you".

I stood there expecting a smile and a hug. My mother's face showed anything but joy. She was not looking at me but over my head. I turned around. My father was standing a few feet behind me with his head hung low. He had tried to catch me before I reached my mother. Mom began to cry and went into the bathroom. The mood in the house was not the joyful Christmas that I had expected. It was sullen and sad. Mom frequently left the room to be alone and though she did her best to hide her feelings, I knew she was crying. Dad left the day after Christmas.

Within a few months, Mom told me that she and Dad were getting divorced. For years I blamed myself for their divorce. If I hadn't been so naïve, if I had just kept my big mouth shut, maybe they would still be married.

George, The Holy Terror

With Dad legally out of the picture and Mom receiving only $50.00/month/child from Dad, life was a struggle. We didn't have a car. The good thing about that was that the bill collectors couldn't tell if Mom was home when they showed up at the door. Leon and I constantly answered the door and the phone telling the bill collectors that Mom wasn't home. Somehow mom managed to pay her bills but seldom at the time they were due.

Around 1957, Mom's mother (Granny) had a major stroke that paralyzed her left side. She came to live with us. The house only had two bedrooms so Mom converted the back porch to a small bedroom and that became her bedroom. She gave the master bedroom to her mother. Granny sold what property she had in Tarboro. With that money and her small retirement funds, life for us was better.

There was a window in our bedroom that originally opened to the back porch. Now it opened to my mother's bedroom. Mom never complained. Now that I'm older, I think back on how she must have looked at her situation in those days.

It had to be tough. She was raising two boys without the help of their father. She had a secretarial job that barely paid the bills. Bill collectors were constantly nipping at her heels. Her invalid mother had come to live with us. Few men would be interested in a woman with all of this baggage no matter how good, smart and attractive the woman. The window between our bedrooms was always closed but some nights, I could hear my mother crying softly. This caused me great frustration and I "acted out".

I became a fighter. When Mom cried, I would fight anyone that crossed my path. It didn't matter how old or how big they were. This gave me some sort of relief and I enjoyed the feeling, win or lose. I probably lost most of those fights ,but I didn't care as long as I got in a few good licks.

I was a good kid and a good student so my constant fighting was frustrating to my teachers, the principal and my mother. One day I was called into the principal's office. The principal, my teachers, the school counselor and my mother were all sitting at a table. In today's terms, this would be called an "intervention". They discussed my fighting and asked me for an explanation. I had none. Everyone except my mother was leaning on putting me in a special school for troubled children.

My mother somehow knew my fighting was connected to her emotions. She told the group what she suspected. She felt that if she kept her emotions under control, maybe I wouldn't fight. That seemed to work for the most part. The number of fights I participated in declined greatly. The problem was that I enjoyed fighting and it didn't take much for me to resort to my old habits.

In those days fights didn't last long and there was seldom any real damage done. Most of my fights after the "Big Meeting" were related to bullying. I was small for my age. My skin was so light that I could be mistaken for being white. My hair looked more like a white person's than a black person's. I was called many names, tripped a lot, and pushed from behind. I soon learned the only way to stop these assaults was to fight.

I had a group of buddies that would indirectly assist me in my fights. Almost all fights took place on the playground at recess or after school. I preferred to fight at recess. Teachers were around so things couldn't get too far out of hand.

If someone was constantly picking on me and I knew I was going to have to fight them, I would gather my buddies and let them know whom I was going to fight. At recess my buddies would remain close by but not so close that they were obvious. I would go very close to the person that was picking on me with the hopes that he would say or do something that I could use as an excuse to fight him. Once he did and the fight was started, everyone on the playground would run to watch it. That's when my buddies would get real close. As long as I was winning, they were to let the fight go on until someone else or a teacher broke it up. If I was getting the worse end of it, they were to break it up immediately.

Once I fought someone, I never had to fight them again. My goal was simple. Inflict enough damage that win or lose, they didn't want to fight me again. I soon had a reputation of being a little crazy and a loose cannon. It was best to leave me alone.

In those days we settled things amongst ourselves. Today kids aren't given that opportunity. Emotions are held in. Bullied kids reach a dangerous point. They may take their own lives or in their frustration, take many lives. Maybe the old way was better.

I was always my mother's protector. When I was very young and Dad wasn't around, some of the neighborhood men would drop by to see if she needed anything. On one occasion that I remember, one of the neighbor men came over. It was obvious that he had been drinking. I could tell that my mother was very uncomfortable and was trying hard to get the neighbor to leave without insulting him. When he approached her, I stepped between them. He could have easily knocked me out of the way, but there was no way I was going to let him touch my mother. He looked at me and smiled. I wasn't smiling back and he could tell I was willing to challenge him if he approached my mother.

To disarm the situation, he told me to be a good boy and get him a glass of water. The kitchen wasn't far away and I had been reared to obey all adults. I went into the kitchen and got a glass of water and a very large kitchen knife. I tucked the knife into the front of my pants leaving the handle exposed. When I handed him the water, I made sure he saw the handle of the knife but kept it out of sight from my mother. He drank the water, took a long hard look at me, and left. He never liked me after that but never came back to the house either.

A Mother's Sacrifice

We lived on the Southwest Side of Durham. Our financial status would probably be classified as "lower middle class" – "upper lower class". As children, my brother and I didn't think much of our financial situation. We always had plenty to eat and nice clothes to wear for school, church and the occasional party. Mom always "laid away" three sets of school clothes and a pair of new shoes for us in the summer.

She managed to pay off the debt by fall so we would have the new clothes by the beginning of school. By switching combinations of paints and shirts we never had to wear the same set in the same week.

One day I realized that our mom was making a tremendous sacrifice so my brother and I could dress well. Mom came home from work at her usual time of 5:30 pm. She was in a rush. She wanted to fix dinner, clean the kitchen, and go to a parent/teachers meeting that night. As she entered the house, I met her at the door and she told me her plans. She was wearing a black dress with short sleeves and a matching short sleeve jacket. She took off the jacket to go to the kitchen and I was appalled.

"Mom", I yelled, "You can't wear that dress. The under arms have rotted away".

She smiled and roughly rubbed her fingers through my hair and said, "It's the only dress I have".

I felt like I had been slapped really hard. I didn't know which was worse, that she only had one dress or that I had never noticed that she was wearing the same dress day in and day out.

From that time on, I began paying attention to my mother and though I was too young to do anything about it then, one day I would see to it that her sacrifices were not in vain.

One of our favorite meals was fried chicken. There were no fast food restaurants in those days and chicken wasn't cut and packaged like it is today. You bought a whole chicken, cleaned it, and cut it into two breast, two thighs, two wings, two legs, and two backs. My mother paid for the chicken, cleaned it, cut it up , and fried it.

When she brought it to the table she would always say, "Save the backs for me. They are my favorite pieces."

The chicken represented two meals. For one meal my brother would get a leg and a breast and I would get a wing and a thigh. The next meal we would reverse our portions. Mom would take one back for each meal.

After the dress incident, I was attuned to her sacrifices and I began taking the backs, leaving a larger piece of meat for her.

She would argue, "I told you to save the backs for me. You know they are my favorite pieces".

I would say, "I like them too". She would smile knowingly and accept my meager offer.

Leon's Brother

Have you ever had someone in your life that was so extraordinary that you paled in existence when you were near him or her? That's how I felt near Leon. Leon was my older brother. He was only one year, one month and 14 days older than I, but several years ahead of me in maturity. Leon hung out with the older, popular kids.

Looking back, I must have had an inferiority complex. I was much more comfortable with kids younger than I. Leon was very handsome, very smart, very athletic, and a great dancer. He knew how to dress to impress. He was not shy around the young ladies and they paid attention to him.

I ,on the other hand, was a good student but somewhat lazy, tried hard, but was not athletically inclined. I was extremely shy around young ladies because I was terrified of rejection and couldn't dance.

Everyone in school knew my brother. If someone asked who I was, another would say, "That's Leon's brother". It happened very often. I began introducing myself that way. I was "Leon's brother". Only my closest associates knew my name was George.

It's funny, after all of these years and my many achievements and somewhat successful life, I will run into an old friend or find someone I knew in high school on Face Book. Before they ask me anything about myself, they'll ask: "Where's Leon"? I don't mind and he will always be my big brother.

So ,before any of you reading this ask, Leon is fine. He lives in Petaluma, CA with his wife Susan (Italian/American). They have two wonderful children, Lucia and a son Leon III. Lucia (at this writing) is married and has a son. Leon is in the real estate business and very active in his church.

My Early Accident-Prone Years

 I was always getting hurt. In kindergarten I fell off the stoop at my school and jammed a wire from a chained link fence through my right shin. I still carry the scar.

When I was eight, I was running around the house and stepped on a milk bottle (Yes! In those days milk came in bottles and was delivered to our front porches), fell, and broke my right arm. The doctor put me in a cast that went from the middle of my palm to just under 3 inches from my shoulder. The cast was set at a right angle and a sling around my neck handled the weight of the cast. The cast was left on for eight weeks.

While wearing the cast, I rode my bike (falling many times), got into many fights (the cast was a formidable weapon) , and played football with the guys in my neighborhood. When I went back to the doctor, my cast had been worn down to the point it no longer kept me from bending my elbow or my wrist. The doctor put me in another cast and warned me to protect the arm or he would "cut the arm off". That scared me to the point that I stayed in the house for the next four weeks.I left only to go to school and back. The arm healed without any complications.

Later in my childhood I was carrying a cane knife (looks like a stick but will pull apart revealing a sharp blade) in my pocket. I tried to snatch it out really fast to show a friend and nearly cut my fingers off. That scar also still adorns my hand.

We roller-skated a lot in my neighborhood. We didn't have fancy rinks or any type of indoor facility. We skated in the street on rough asphalt. Our skates were metal and were not part of our shoes. We had to wear hard sole shoes so the skates could be clipped on to the front soles of our shoes with a metal curvature.

That metal contraption had to be tightened with a skate key that hung from a shoestring around your neck for easy access. A strap from the back of the skate went around the ankles and was fastened with a buckle. It was fairly common to see someone's skates detach from that front metal clip on one foot. This would cause the skate to swing wildly around the ankle of the poor skater as he/she hopped on one leg and skated with the other foot trying to regain control before the free swinging skate tripped him/her. I would wager you that we surviving adults still bare the strap marks, scared knees, hands , and elbows from those occasions. I have many healed cuts and abrasions from the multiple accidents I've had over those years.

The neighborhood I grew up in was blessed with boys my own age. We played baseball, basketball and my favorite, football. The only protective equipment that adorned our fragile bodies was our courage and the belief of invulnerability. I was very small for my age but had nerves of steel. One day we were playing football with some visiting kids that outsized us by quiet a bit. They chose to run most of their plays right through the part of the line that I was supposed to defend. After about six straight times of literally running over me, I decided it would not happen again.

As the runner charged my area of the line , I braced my-self and got as low as I could. When the runner approached, I grabbed him around his legs and lifted with all of the strength I could muster. I lifted him straight up in the air and at the peak of the lift, my legs gave out and he fell on top of me. My head landed on a rock pressed to my temple. The weight of the runner falling on me drove my temple down on the rock and it punctured my head.

My teammates were cheering the great tackle I had made, but I didn't get up. I was in severe pain and was trying not to cry. I was holding my right hand to the right side of my head when someone rolled me over. They all jumped back and someone hollered, "His brains are coming out". I looked at my hand and it was holding a large blood clot. I really thought it was my brains and howled like a banshee.

I was rushed to the hospital. The whole side of my head was shaved. The wound was cleaned and sutured. A bandage was wrapped around and around my head. I looked like a soldier returning from the war. A week later I returned to the hospital to have the sutures removed. The doctor removed the bandage and looked at my head. He said the wound was healing well, but the hair will probably not grow back. He meant the hair directly over the small scar on my hairline. I thought he meant the whole side of my head that had been shaved when the wound was cleaned. I howled like a wounded cat. The doctor was amazed. I hadn't made a peep when he cleaned and sutured my wound and now I was carrying on like a baby.

Snake Bite

I loved to walk in the woods and catch tadpoles salamanders, turtles, and snakes. One freakishly warm spell in December lasted several weeks during my early teens. I went walking in the woods during the evening wearing a short sleeve shirt and a jacket tied around my waist. I was a good ways from home when I felt something hard and sharp hit the back of my right hand. I dismissed the incident as a brier bush and continued my walk.

Five minutes latter my hand began to throb. I looked at my hand and it was swollen to twice its normal size. There were two puncture marks about a ½ inch apart. The marks were typical of fang marks from a venomous snake. My knowledge of snakes alerted me to the importance of identifying the snake so the proper anti-venom could be administered.

I used my belt as a tourniquet and quickly retraced my steps. I found a bush with a three-foot long copperhead snake coiled in the branches. I picked up a stick, clubbed the snake out of the bush , and continued my attack until I was sure it was dead. I put my jacket on and stuffed the dead snake in a pocket. I half ran and half walked. I was afraid running would increase my circulatory rate and the venom would reach my heart at a quicker rate. Walking too slowly may cause me to pass out before I reached help. No one knew where I was.

I reached home and rushed into my house and into the kitchen where Mom was about to start dinner. I told her I had been snake bit and needed to go to the hospital. Mom knew I had a better than average knowledge of snakes and wouldn't joke about a matter like that. She also knew I was deathly afraid of needles and would never want to be taken to a hospital unless it was truly an emergency. We didn't own a car so a neighbor was called and together we rushed to the hospital.

When we entered the hospital, my mother told the nurse at admissions that a snake had bitten me. The nurse went into panic mode and was rushing around trying to find out whom to call.

I was eventually led into a doctor's office where the doctor sat calmly behind his desk with a pipe hanging from his mouth. He wore horn-rimmed glasses. He peered at me over the top of his glasses and said, "Son, don't you know snakes hibernate in the winter?"

I reached in my jacket pocket, grabbed the dead snake, and tossed it on his desk as I replied, "That one didn't."

I've never seen a grown man jump so fast. He knocked over his chair and joined his nurse in panic mode. It was obvious they had never dealt with a snakebite before.

I was hospitalized. It was decided that since snakes are warm blooded and hibernate in the winter months, this snake had come out because of the freakishly warm weather. Since it had been fairly inactive, most likely it had not developed enough venom to harm me. The decision was made to keep me for observation.

I was given a list of symptoms that occurred from a venomous snakebite. I was instructed that if any of these symptoms occurred, I was to alert the nurse so they could start a series of anti-venom injections.

During the night, I experienced every symptom (real or imagined) that the doctor described, but I was more afraid of needles than of the consequences of the snakebite.

When the nurses checked on me and asked how I was feeling, I was quick to answer, "Just fine."

The Daisy Eagle

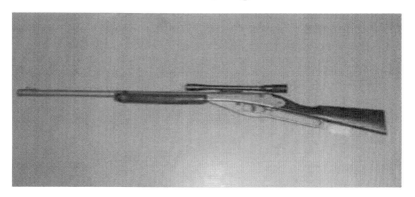

The BB rifle was my favorite toy. My brother and I were the envy of the neighborhood because we had "Daisy Eagle" BB rifles instead of the standard "Red Rider" BB rifles. The Daisy Eagle came with an adjustable scope and a paint finish that made it look golden. The rifles could hold about 25 BBs. We filled them by pouring the BB's in our mouth and spitting them down a small holding tube under the rifles barrel.

My brother and I were not allowed to have the rifles loaded in the house. We opened the holding barrel and poured the BBs out each night. That would clear the BBs from the cylinder. We would shake the rifle and listen for the sound of a rolling BB. If we heard none , we were fairly certain the gun was unloaded.

One evening after dinner, I was lying on my bed with my "unloaded" Daisy Eagle. I was sighting different things in my room through the rifle's scope. I finally focused on Pete, our blue, male parakeet. He was sitting on his perch with his head cocked to the side in his usual curious way. I slowly squeezed the trigger of my supposedly empty rifle and the rifle fired. Pete fell to the floor of his cage. I jumped up and ran to the cage. Pete wasn't breathing. I realized that I had cocked the rifle before I emptied the cylinder. This put a BB in the firing chamber and it wouldn't make a sound when the rifle was shaken.

I quickly put the rifle in its rack, put the cover over Pete's cage, and cut off the lights in my bedroom. The next morning I got up after a restless night. I dressed, ate breakfast, got my books , and hurried off to school.

After school I returned to my room. Pete's cage was still covered and undisturbed. I changed my clothes and hurried out to the neighborhood basketball court. I didn't come home till dinnertime. I ate the meal my mother had prepared in silence. I went to my room to do my homework.

My mother came in to see if I needed any help. She noticed Pete's cage was still covered. Before I could react, she approached the cage and pulled the cover off. I heard Pete squawk. I jumped up and ran to the cage. Pete was on his perch looking around, surprised at the sudden disturbance. I was speechless. The BB had probably grazed him or knocked the wind out of him , but there he was alive and well. I never pointed anything at Pete again.

Most of the kids in our neighborhood had BB rifles. We shot at targets and sometimes each other. We especially shot at kids that weren't from our neighborhood. We had an unwritten code. If you had a bead on someone with your rifle and they weren't aware of your presence, you had to warn them to allow them a chance to give up or run before you fired a shot.

Our neighborhood was near the forest and I loved to hide among the trees, waiting for an unsuspecting target. One time I spent all day building a platform up in a tree that over looked a well-used path through the woods. When it was complete, I climbed up in it and laid flat, waiting for someone to come by. Eventually three boys from the project came by. They all had BB rifles.

When they were directly under me, I took aim at one of them and shouted out a warning, "Give up or I'll fire". They looked up and saw me on my platform.

They accessed the situation and split up and shouted, "We don't give up". They started shooting. Their aim was deadly. They hit any part of me that protruded from the platform. Since I was surrounded, anytime I rose even a little to try to get a shot at one of them, I exposed myself to two other deadly shooters. They finally got bored or ran out of ammunition and left. I never tried that stunt again.

When there was a conflict with one of the neighboring boys, instead of fighting, we had duels. My brother and I had single shot BB pistols. To fire a shot, you placed a BB in your mouth. You pressed a switch on the barrel of the pistol and the barrel broke down on a hinge. You then placed your BB in the barrel, closed the barrel, removed the safety, and cocked the pistol. Now you could fire one shot.

One day Joe and I got into an argument. We decided to settle it with a duel. All of the neighborhood kids turned out to watch the duel. We went to a construction site at the end of the street so none of our parents would see us. The workers had left for the day.

We got in the middle of the road back to back and stepped off ten paces as one of the boys counted off the steps. We each had a pistol and one BB in our mouth. When we reached ten paces, we both turned. Joe was nervous and was rushing to get the first shot. I was taking my time. I had been in many of these duels and the rule was we both had to stand there until each of us had fired our shot.

Joe rushed through the process and fired quickly, hitting me in my right thigh. I didn't even flinch. I continued loading my gun and when I was through, I took slow aim at various parts of his body. Joe was irritated with having to stand there as I tortured him with methodical aiming.

He finally said, "Shoot or I'm leaving". At that point he made a break for a large stack of bricks and hid behind them.

I shouted, "No fair. You have to let me get my shot".

Joe peeked out from behind the bricks and shouted back, "You had your chance and didn't take it".

I threw down my pistol and grabbed my Daisy Eagle. I watched as Joe peeked out from behind the bricks. I saw where his head was and took careful aim at that spot. The next time he peeked out, I fired.

Joe slammed his hand over his left eye and screamed. I dropped my rifle and ran home. Our parents had warned us time and time again not to shoot at anybody. You might put their eye out.

I stayed in the house all weekend and shook like a leaf every time the phone rang. The following Monday as the kids gathered to walk to school, I saw Joe but he didn't have any type of bandage over his eye. I did see that he had a mark the size of a BB on the side of his nose just a fraction of an inch from his eye. I never shot my BB gun at anything but targets after that.

World's Fastest Skater

We lived on Rosewood Street in Durham, NC. The street had sections added to it over the years, but originally it was a long hill divided into two blocks by Lawson Street (a busy street in those days). Leon was a great skater and won most of the races in the neighborhood. Somehow we decided we would set the "World Fastest Speed Skating Record". Rosewood Street was the perfect place because of its long hill. We owned a huge but friendly boxer dog named "Major".

We kept Major chained in the back yard so he wouldn't run all over the neighborhood. For this occasion, Major and his chain were brought to the top of the hill. One end of the chain was clipped to Major's collar. The other end went around Leon's waist. We sent a "look out" to the busy intersection to watch for cars. I was half a block down the 1st hill halfway between the intersection and my brother. I had a large bone. Major was being held by Leon at the top of the hill.

When the "intersection lookout" hollered, "All clear", everything happened at once.

I showed Major the bone and called him. Leon let go of Major's collar. Major took off down the hill trying to catch me. Leon was jerked almost off of his feet but managed to keep his balance. He was being pulled down the hill at an alarming speed. I stole a glance back as I ran down the hill. Major was running fast and picking up speed as he chased me down the hill. Leon was hanging on to the chain for dear life. His face was frozen with fear. The friction from his skates and the street made a funnel of sparks trailing behind him.

As I approached the intersection, the lookout hollered, "Bus coming".

I could see the bus approaching and it was going to arrive just in time to hit my dog, my brother or both. There was absolutely no way to stop them in time. I accessed my options and without hesitation, made a U turn and started running back up the hill. Major followed my lead and trailed behind me. Leon was franticly trying to unloosen the chain from around his waist but it was securely fastened. Leon continued down the hill at an unbelievable speed. Major and I were going in the opposite direction.

When that chained pulled tight, both Major and Leon were snatched off of their feet. Both hollered and hit the street with a thunderous sound. I rushed to my dog (the early vet in me) to make sure he was all right. He had the wind knocked out of him but he was OK. My quick thinking had saved both. Oh, by the way, Leon was OK also. I wonder if he still has those chain marks.

48

My Short Sand Lot Football Career

When I was in high school, I had a run in with one of the boys in my neighborhood. Russ was much larger than the rest of us and was always in trouble in school and at home. His mother lied to the army recruiter so he could join the Army. She told them he was 18 years old when he was really sixteen. After he finished basic training, he came home on leave. He was big when he left but now he was enormous. His neck was like a wedge. He told us he played football on the Army's team. This couldn't be true. He had just finished basic training and had not been in the service long enough to be on their football team.

I didn't believe him. I always had a big mouth and frequently got in a trouble over my head by sounding off before I thought things through. A big mouth had consequences in those days.

I said, "You couldn't play before you left. What makes you think that we believe you can play now?".

There was dead silence. One of the kids then decided on a contest to determine if Russ was the great football player he claimed to be. All of the kids were to form two lines facing each other forming a narrow passage. Russ was at one end of the passage of boys and I was at the other. Russ had a football and was going to run down that passage. I was to tackle him .To this day I don't understand how that would determine Russ' athleticism. He outweighed me by a hundred pounds. Maybe this was set up to punish me more than it was to show Russ up.

Anyway we got into our positions. I knew I was going to get creamed. My only thought was to stay strong, show no fear , and pray that I would survive. The signal was given and Russ was coming, gaining speed with every step. I was terrified. Russ was huge and I knew I couldn't stop him.

Just as he reached me, I lost my nerve. I raised my right arm to cover my head in an effort to protect that vital part of me from the punishment that was sure to come. At that very instance, Russ had mercy on me and tried to jump over me.

My raised arm caught his toe as he was trying to clear me. Thinking he was going to fall on me, I stood up carrying his legs high in the air. Russ turned a somersault in mid air and landed on his back with a tremendous thud. The impact shook the ground and knocked the wind out of Russ. He was lying on his back, gasping for air like a gold fish out of water.

 I took full advantage of an unexpected opportunity. I stood over him, pounded my chest, and said with a thunderous voice, "Get up and try again!"

The spectators, who had been stunned into a silent gasp at the unexpected turn of event, suddenly broke out in a loud cheer. They were in awe of my heroic feat. They congratulated me and patted me on the back. For the next few weeks, I was the first one chosen when teams were picked for football.

Granny

When I was in my teens, Granny (my maternal grandmother) had a major stroke that left her left side paralyzed for life. She could no longer take care of herself so she sold her property in Tarboro and came to live with us.

We had a TV. This was in the very early days of television and color television was not yet available. We had three channels and TV signed off at 9 pm.

I don't know if the stroke affected Granny's mind or that she just couldn't grasp the idea of how a TV worked but she had some strange ideas. Granny thought that if she were watching a program and needed to go to the bathroom, all she had to do was cut the TV off. It then would resume from the same spot when she returned and cut it back on. She accused my brother and me of tampering with the TV when this didn't happen (this was many decades before you could pause a program).

Mom bought customized, floor length drapes for the living room and dining room. This was quite an event for our family. We didn't have a lot of money so buying something new was cause for a celebration.

Granny's favorite show was a variety show called "The Ed Sullivan Show". Ed was the host and introduced America to a variety of talents for an hour. The show was on every Sunday at 7 pm. Granny would sit in front of that set and could not be moved while The Ed Sullivan Show was on.

The Sunday following the purchase of mom's new drapes, Granny and I were in the dining room waiting for "The Ed Sullivan Show." She watched for ten minutes then struggled to get out of her chair. She made her way over to the TV set and cut it off.

I was startled and said, "Granny! That's "The Ed Sullivan Show."

She said, "I know what it is."

I said, "But that's your favorite show".

She said, "Not any more ". She paused for a minute and then continued, "That man has been coming into our house every Sunday evening for as long as I can remember. If he doesn't have manners enough to say something nice about your mama's new drapes, I'm not going to let him back in".

Granny was getting larger and larger. One day while watching TV, she saw an advertisement for Metrecal. This was supposedly a miracle product that would melt away your fat. You were supposed to eat two Metrecal wafers for breakfast and lunch instead of your regular breakfast and lunch foods. You could eat a light dinner and drink a Metrical shake with your final meal. Your weight was suppose to melt away.

Granny had mom buy her a supply of this amazing new product. After weeks of watching, granny ate everything she had always eaten along with her metrical wafers and shakes, I finally said to her, "Granny , you are suppose to use the wafers and shakes as a substitute for food- not eat any thing you want and the wafers and shake too. You'll never lose weight the way you're doing it".

Granny glared at me and said, "That's what you think, Mr. Smarty Pants." She stood with some difficulty and said, "Look at how loose my housecoat is on me."

She did a slow pirouette to show the loose fitting housecoat. As she turned, she also exposed the ruptured seam up the back of her housecoat that had burst from the pressure of her girth.

Meeting My Future Wife Natalie

When I was 12 years old, Leon showed me a picture of a girl in his class. I thought this was the prettiest girl I had ever seen. Leon told me her name was Wanda Jean and that she had a sister named Natalie that was in my grade (6th grade). Next year, we would be in the same school.

I told him, "That's the girl I'm going to marry"..

He told Wanda Jean what I had said about marrying her sister and of course she told Natalie.

Natalie was furious. She had never met me and was certain she didn't like me.

The next year, we were not only in the same grade, we were in the same homeroom class. I wasn't disappointed. I thought she was beautiful (I still do). I was very shy and wouldn't dare approach her. It was just as well. She knew who I was and had already decided she wasn't going to like me. So I just admired her from a distance for the next three years.

Everyone knew I had a tremendous crush on Natalie and teased me constantly. We were probably in junior high school before I had nerve enough to approach Nat. I asked to carry her books home. She gave me her books and I struggled to carry both her books and mine.

She didn't walk with me. She walked ahead of me with friends from her neighborhood (she still to this day tries to walk ahead of me). I would give her books back to her when we reached her house and anxiously await the next day when I could do it all again.

She tried avoiding me by running into the girl's bathroom or hiding behind classmates when she saw me coming. I was undaunted and would be patiently waiting whenever she decided to immerge from the bathroom or from behind her classmates.

From the 10th -11th grade, I only had nerve enough to call her once. I asked what girls liked to talk about.

She said, "Clothes and cooking". I knew nothing about any of those things so I never called back.

When we were in our senior year, we went to school dances and house parties. I was extremely shy and didn't know how to dance to fast tunes. I probably should have asked Nat to teach me but never did. I would go to the dances, sit with Nat, and watch others dance. I could only dance with her on the slow records. Usually friends would stop by and ask Nat for a dance on the fast songs. She danced well and I didn't really mind. I was afraid that if I attempted to fast dance, everyone would stare at me and some may even laugh. I went through high school without learning to dance.

One winter evening Nat and I were leaving a house party that had steep steps leading from the front porch to the street. As we stepped outside to leave, we realized the cold rain that had been falling when we arrived had now formed a sheet of ice covering the walkway and steps.

We made if off the porch and down the sidewalk. I held Nat's hand tightly as we reached the first set of steps. We slipped on the first step and slid down the whole flight of steps on our behinds. When we finally hit bottom, I was still holding Nat's hand. Maybe if I had let go, I could have stopped or slowed our decent. By trying to be chivalrous or protective, I never let her go. Today we are in our 60's, we've been married over 46 years and in each other's lives for 58 years. I still haven't let go.

Nat and I are very connected. Several years ago we took a course offered in our church titled "Finding Your God Given

Gifts". The moderator said God has given all of us certain gifts. Some are easily recognized. Others are subtler. Some are given many gifts and some just one. Most of us go through life without ever knowing our gift(s). He also informed us that this course would not necessarily identify our gifts, but give us a method to use in trying to identify them for ourselves.

The course consisted of four sessions, three hours long. They were given at our church on Saturdays for four weeks. Nat and I attended all of the sessions.

At the end of the final session, the moderator asked us to do something that had nothing to do with our God given gifts. He asked us to write down on a sheet of paper, the five most important events in our lives. It could come from childhood, teen years, school or adulthood.

He then asked us to place the five events in the order of importance with the most important listed first and the least, last.

Natalie and I were sitting on opposite ends of the room , but listed the exact same events and placed them in the exact same order.

The moderator was astonished. He had never had any couple do anything like this in all of his years. There is no explanation for this. If you asked us to do it again, we would probably list different things but on that day at that moment we were on one accord. It was also so the last time we were on one accord about anything.

Rock Star

I joined a rock and roll band called the "Viceroys" when I was in the 10th grade. I was a year older than the other members. Our musicians played trumpet, saxophone, bass guitar, trombone, and drums. I played lead guitar and was mediocre at best. The other guys were very talented.

There were several bands in the area competing for gigs (jobs). Each band had some gimmick to set them apart from the other bands. All of our band members could play multiple instruments. This was during the time when the limbo was popular. For you reading youngsters, the limbo was a calypso song that when played, two people would hold either end of a long stick and dancers would dance under the stick. When all dancers had gone under, the stick was lowered and the dancers would pass under the stick again. If you hit the stick or fell, you had to get out of the limbo line. This would continue until there was only one remaining dancer. He or she was cheered and made limbo king or queen for the day.

Our band would start playing a limbo tune and our band members formed a limbo line. As the trumpeter reached the stick, he tossed his trumpet back. I would catch it and start playing it as I tossed my guitar back when I reached the stick. The drummer caught the guitar and played and so on and so on. The crowds loved it and no other band could match our gimmick. This was an expensive gimmick because sometimes we dropped an instrument. We mainly played in nightclubs (we were under age by today's standards) and fraternity parties. Our parents only allowed us to play on Friday and Saturday nights. We became very popular with the college crowd and had no trouble getting work. In school we played for dances, proms , and half time shows at basketball games.

Our band purchased a used six-door limousine (Plymouth). One of the fathers had to drive because none of us was old enough to drive. We played from Washington, DC to Atlanta, GA. We had a great time and met some of the biggest stars of our time.

One night we were playing at a small club in Raleigh, NC. The club was sparsely filled. I noticed a thin black man closely watching us. He seemed to focus on my guitar playing technique. There was a young, well -endowed woman sitting with him that appeared bored with everything. When our band took a break, the man approached me and asked if he and his woman could sing a song for the audience during this break. He also wanted to use my guitar. I had no problem with it so I told him to go ahead without asking the management or our bandleader.

As I walked to the rest area, I heard my guitar scream as it never had before. The man was pounding out a rhythm that had the audience immediately on their feet. The man introduced himself and his wife- Ike and Tina Turner. He also introduced their latest song, not yet released, "Proud Mary".

When he finished his song, he announced he and Tina were playing a few blocks away and invited our audience to follow them. They did. The owner of the club was furious with me. He paid us a portion of what we were promised and sent us packing. We went to the club where Ike and Tina were performing. When Ike saw us, he invited us to join his band and play with him for the night. We did and now we have a tale to tell our grand children.

I also worked in my uncle's drug store. The only hotel for blacks in Durham was above his drug store. All of the black entertainers and sport figures that came to Durham stayed in that hotel. Many of them came to the drug store for cigarettes, sodas, candy or medication. I waited on a lot of them. I never thought to ask for an autograph.

PART THREE

College Days

Tuskegee, One Year and Out

After the 12th grade, I went to Tuskegee to study Pre-Veterinary Medicine. Natalie stayed in Durham. Duke University decided to accept their first black students the summer of our high school graduation. Natalie was one of two students chosen from our high school to join three other minority students to integrate Duke University. Her father said, "NO!" So Natalie enrolled at North Carolina College and majored in mathematics. She received a full four year academic scholarship.

I had also received an academic scholarship to Tuskegee Institute. My major was in pre-veterinary medicine. This was my first time away from home and my mother's supervision.

No one at Tuskegee knew me. I was now in a situation completely new to me. I was an unknown commodity. I could totally redefine my personality. No one knew I was shy, immature, and couldn't dance. At that time, I didn't smoke drink or curse. All of that changed.

I became aggressively friendly, especially to the young ladies. I joined the swimming team and a freshman rock band. When the opportunity presented itself, I danced all night long. I loved dancing and wasn't half bad. I learned all of the latest steps and made up a few new ones.

As a first year college student, I was very naïve. My fellow students enjoyed taking advantage of my less than worldly knowledge. On my first trip to Tuskegee, I was treated to my first train ride. The first leg of the trip was from Durham to Atlanta. When the train reached Atlanta, the conductor told all of students going to Tuskegee to move to the car at the end of the train. This was in 1963 and segregation was still the norm in the Deep South. I was in Georgia going to Alabama. My immediate thought was that this was an act of southern racism.

One of the students, noticing my perplexed facial expression, explained. The closest station to Tuskegee was in a town called Chee Haw. He said the train wouldn't stop in Chee Haw but the conductor would slow the train down, uncouple the last car, and let it coast to a stop. He was pulling my leg. The train did stop.

When we de-boarded the train, I got the shock of my life. Chee Haw was like an old western train station. There was a small building badly in need of repair. It had no train station personnel. We de-boarded and received our luggage. Everyone but me seemed to have a ride to Tuskegee. Dumb me just stood there as , one by one, everyone left the station. Eventually, I was totally alone - no telephone, no taxi, nothing. My eyes filled with water. I wanted to go home. After 15 minutes of self pity, a green limousine pulled up. The driver asked if I was a Tuskegee student. I answered yes. He apologized for being late and informed me that he always met the trains. He loaded my luggage in the limousine and drove me to my dormitory in style. It was a freshman dorm. I made quite an impression arriving in a chauffeured limousine.

My first days in a dorm at Tuskegee were lonely. I was homesick and bored. When I unpacked, I found my mother had placed a book "Valley of the Dolls" in my suitcase. I began to read it that evening and I was hooked. I had never read a novel that was not a school assignment until that moment. From that point on, I became an avid reader. I love reading about history, science fiction, horror, and just about anything.

I also missed Natalie. I began writing to her on a weekly basis and cherishing the letters she wrote to me.

My first trip back to Durham meant going back to Chee Haw and catching the train. I was told that the train wouldn't stop at Chee Haw unless I flagged it down. When I asked how to flag down a train, my new "friends" smiled. They told me to take the sheet off of my bed and catch a taxi to Chee Haw. When I heard the train coming, I was to stand in the middle of the tracks and start flapping that sheet as hard as I could. That would signal the train conductor to stop.

When the students saw me take a sheet off of my bed, they leveled with me. There was a lantern with a swinging handle at the station. I was to light the lantern and swing it outward toward the track and the conductor would stop. That worked fine but from that moment on, I caught the bus home and back.

I joined the swimming team and turned out to be a pretty good athlete. I swam the 100m freestyle, 200m freestyle, 500m freestyle, 400m freestyle re-lay, and 400m individual medley. Only two freshmen made the team that year. The other had received a swimming scholarship. I was a "walk on"
.

I had never competed on a swimming team before. I was an unlikely candidate for a swimmer. Most swimmers were tall and sleek with long arms and legs. I stood only five feet, six inches. I had to take three strokes for every two strokes by the taller swimmers just to go the same distance. My skills were very rough and amateurish, but I was fast and had endurance.

The coach was pretty hard on the other freshman. He was in school on a swimming scholarship and I was the better swimmer. As the coach smoothed out my swimming technique, I became a threat in any free style event. I had a very fast start and never seemed to tire so I finished strong.

I would intentionally lay back in a distance race until the last two lapses. Then I would pick up my pace. I could hear the crowd react. I would sprint to the finish and more times than not, win in the last few seconds.

My coach fussed at me and said if I had that much energy left at the end of the race, I should swim harder during the middle stretch. I never changed my technique and our team was SEAC champion that year and I was a star.

I was truly enjoying the college experience at Tuskegee. I had the social life I had always dreamed of but my grades were horrible.

I was from a school that boasted 240 seniors and was in college with kids that only had seven or eight seniors in their high school class. The work wasn't hard or beyond my knowledge. I just didn't go to class. I was enjoying the college experience.

By the end of my freshman year, I had taken 38 hours worth of course credits and had D's and F's in all but 11 credits. Natalie on the other hand had made all A's except for a B in Physical Education (a course worth only one hour of credit).

Tuskegee dropped my scholarship and sent me a letter that summer saying that if I would return for summer school and make at least a 3.0 average in summer courses, they would consider letting me come back the following fall.

I was devastated. My mother was disappointed in me and that troubled me more than anything. I seriously thought about not going back to school. I toyed with the idea of joining the Army.

When I mentioned this idea to Natalie she said, "You've wanted to be a veterinarian every since I've known you. That's what you ought to be".

I told my mother that I was going back to Tuskegee. She gave me an alternative. She was acting dean of admissions at NCC. She told me she would give me the same opportunity Tuskegee had offered. She would let me enroll in NCC's summer school. If I earned a 3.0 grade point in summer school, she would allow me to enroll in the fall semester. She told me she would see to it that I had a bed to sleep in and food to eat, but as far as my school expenses, I would have to pay for them myself.

This was great. I would save lots of money by staying at home. Best of all, I would be near Natalie. I enrolled in summer school and worked all summer to get enough money for the fall semester.

I worked very hard in school and in the industrial world for the next three years. I taught swimming to the PE Majors. I was lifeguard for recreational swimming and I had a lab job at night at the VA Hospital. I took as large a course load as the college would allow and I made the dean's list every semester. I had to make up 29 hours to graduate with my rightful class so I took courses in both sessions of summer school each summer of my college years. By the end of my senior year, I had more than made up the credit deficits. Meanwhile, Natalie was aceing every class. She graduated top of our class with a 3.999 grade point. I had a respectable 3.383.

Three good things came out of that horrible academic performance at Tuskegee.

1) While in Tuskegee, Cassius Clay (heavy weight boxer) stopped on campus. He was on his way to Florida to fight Sonny Liston (the world's heavy weight champion). He arrived in a long black limousine. He opened the roof, stood up so we could see him, and hollered, "Is this the place they sell peanuts "(a play on the fact that George Washington Carver saved the South's cotton plantations by developing the peanut as an alternative crop. He developed hundreds of ways to use every potion of the peanut in his Tuskegee laboratory).

Word of Cassius Clay's presence on campus spread like wildfire. The gym was opened so we could meet and talk with him. I was able to get his autograph. After the fight with Liston, Clay was the new heavy weight champion. He changed his name to Mohammad Ali. I probably have one of the last autographs he signed as Cassius Clay.

2) Natalie and I had begun corresponding with each other through letters. I could put on paper what I couldn't say to her face. We were becoming boyfriend and girlfriend through letters.

3) Transferring to NCC had an added bonus. By switching schools, all of my passing grades turned to credits. The failing grades would not transfer so they disappeared and did not count against my new grade point. The slate was wiped clean and I had a fresh start in the academic grade point world.

If I had gone back to Tuskegee, all of those bad grades would have kept my grade point so low that I would have never been accepted into the graduate program of Veterinary Medicine.

My Years At NCCU

I worked very hard at NCCU. I was a biology major and chemistry minor. Between schoolwork and working three part time jobs, I had very little time for social life. Natalie and I were very much in love at this time. I didn't have to worry about her showing interest in other young men. She was truly loyal. We both studied during the weekdays, but still managed to eat lunch together most days.

The first job I had only paid me $18.00/month. We would take her car to Hardee's everyday. Hardee's was our first fast food restaurant and it was strictly carry out. A hamburger cost $0.15 and a drink was a dime. There was no food tax in those days. I could feed her for $0.25. I prayed that she didn't want french fries. That would mean I would have to go without my hamburger.

We saw each other every weekend. As I took on more jobs, our dating progressed. Dating consisted of going to parties, an occasional movie and on special occasions, going out to dinner.

I remember one special evening I carried Nat to a restaurant in Chapel Hill. It was a very popular place for UNC students. You had to leave main street, go down an ally and there was the entrance to Rathskeller's.

I asked to be seated in the "Cave". This special section in the restaurant had walls that had been made to look like the inside of a cave. Lamps leaned out from the walls. The effect was far different from anything Nat had ever experienced.

Our waiter, a young black man about our age, showed us to our table. Before we were seated, Nat asked to use the powder room. Our waiter politely showed her the way.

When she returned to our seat, she had a strange look on her face. When I asked her what was the matter, she embarrassingly handed me a note. Our waiter had slipped the note into her hand. It had his name and phone number on it.

I took the note and showed no sign that I had seen it as our waiter served us with exuberance. The meal was delicious. When we finished our meal, I left him his note under my plate instead of a tip.

Our professors at NCC were hard but fair. Some of them took joy in terrorizing their students. One such Professor was Dr. Mary Towns, head of the Department of Biology.

Dr. Towns was ambidextrous and could write very fast. The first day in class, she introduced herself by facing the board and writing as she spoke. She had the chalk in her left hand as she spoke and wrote, "My name is Doctor". At this point, in a very smooth motion, she switched the chalk to her right hand and picked up the eraser with her left hand. She continued talking as she wrote but was now erasing her previous writing, "Mary Towns". Then she began her lecture, writing with her right hand as fast as she talked and erasing with her left hand. It was something to behold.

Dr. Vernon Clark was my favorite biology professor. He was young, dedicated, and single. He asked me to join his research team of young promising students.

We volunteered to assist him in the laboratory work he needed to complete his PhD. from Duke University. These were segregated times and although he had been admitted to Duke's Graduate Program and although he proved to be an exceptionally gifted student, they had no intention of giving him a PhD from Duke University.

He refused to let them discourage him and held fast. It took him much longer than it should have ,but he showed them he would not quit nor be discouraged. He eventually got his PhD.

Dr. Clark was working on "The Electrophoretic Analysis of Lactic Dehydrogenase". Working with Dr. Clark changed my lackluster attitude toward learning and I became a very good student.

Natalie graduated with the highest grade point in our class and was given a teaching fellowship for a Masters degree in mathematics at the University of Michigan. I graduated with respectable grades and was accepted into Tuskegee Institute University's, School of Veterinary Medicine.

The summer was bitter sweet. Natalie and I had become inseparable ,but we knew we would be separated by over a 1000 miles at summer's end. The summer ended and we both went our separate ways.

My Years As A Student Of Veterinary Medicine

The first day of my freshman year, I was sitting in the auditorium with the other 41 freshmen of my class. The Dean of the Vet School strolled in. He was a tall, thin, distinguished looking man. He starred at us for a few minutes as if to size us up.

Then he spoke, "Look at the person sitting to your left".

I thought his next statement would be, "Introduce yourself and tell him/her where you're from".

Instead he said, "One of you won't be here next year".

That statement scared the crap out of me. I later learned that Tuskegee's Veterinary School had a policy of washing out 50% of each class regardless of grade point by the end of the sophomore year.

Our class was very diverse. We had six African American men, four African American women, four white men, one white woman and the rest were from Africa and Caribbean Islands.

This was a wonderful experience for all of us. I don't recall any major racial instances in the four years most of us spent together. All of the white students were from the North and chose to live off campus. I'm sure it was a different experience for them to be the minority race in any situation.

I lived on campus and was assigned to a room with another African American freshman veterinary student. He was older than I. He had finished college and served in the military. At the age of 20, I was the youngest student in my class.

Our classes weren't difficult but the tests were intense. We were required to know the material in depth. We developed study groups that for the most part were racially divided. I guess for this type of intense studying we sought a comfort zone. We were reluctant to show any weakness to a different racial group.

Our group was made up of four of the six African American males. Ralph would not join our group. He wanted to study alone. This was his second effort at Tuskegee's Vet School. He had failed his first attempt and wouldn't be given another chance if he failed again. Ralph studied all of the time. Unfortunately, he couldn't retain the information.

One late Saturday night, half way through our first semester, I returned to the dormitory from a party. As I walked down the long hallway to my room, I saw Ralph approaching me in a strange manner. He didn't seem to notice me as he approached. I stopped and watched him. He was walking in slow motion with his head held down and moving slowly forward but also moving from one side of the wall to the other. He was reaching up and touching each wall as high as he could reach. I watched until he was only about ten feet from me.

I said, "What-cha doing Ralph?"

He looked up startled at first and then smiled. He said, "I was once a little baby. First I learned to crawl and then I learned to walk. Each step I take brings me closer to death. Sooo, I'm taking my time."

I was concerned and thought Ralph was either on some sort of drug or had lost his mind. I told him he was studying too hard and needed to relax a little.

He said, "No! I don't deserve any rest. I need to keep studying."

The following morning, the school ambulance was in front of our dorm. They were taking Ralph away. Ralph never returned to class and after he was released from the school hospital, he left for his parents' home in Virginia. That was a wakeup call for the rest of my class. Studying was important, but we also needed to relax and take some personal time to refresh our minds.

My roommate moved to a rental house for more room and more privacy. I was assigned another roommate. He was the other African American that didn't study in our group. He became very involved with a young lady in undergrad school and began neglecting his work.

 I became very concerned about him and talked to his girlfriend. I warned her that her boyfriend was in danger of failing his freshman year if he didn't pick up his grades. I asked her if she would encourage him to work harder.

He found out that I had talked to his girlfriend about his private matters and became very angry with me. He demanded that I stay out of his business. I respected his wishes and left him to his fate.

He washed out by the end of our freshman year. School was very demanding and we had little or no time for social pleasures.

During our first year apart, Natalie and I wrote to each other constantly and called when we could. My plan for Natalie and myself was that I would marry her the summer after my sophomore year. I wanted to wait until then because I didn't want any distractions that could cause me to drop to that lower 50% of my class.

Nat and I both returned to Durham during our Christmas break but only had a week together (my school was on the semester system and Nat's was on a trimester system). I was home a week before Natalie, but left a week before she had to return to Michigan.

Before Nat arrived I had confided in my mother that I wanted to ask Nat to marry me on Christmas day. I told her of my plans to marry her the summer after my sophomore year.

Mom told me Nat's father was very old school and that I needed to show him respect by asking his permission to marry his daughter.

He was a big man that didn't talk much but when he did it was with force and authority. He was a very intimidating man.

I went to Nat's house and told Nat's mother that I intended to ask her husband for Nat's hand in marriage. She knew I was nervous, so she gave me a big glass of scotch. After I had emptied the glass, she sent me to the kitchen to talk with Nat's father.

He was sitting at the kitchen table, watching a football game on a small TV set and listening to another on his radio.

I asked if I could speak with him. He turned the sound down on his devices and gave me his full attention.

I told him that Natalie and I had been dating for a good while and we were very much in love with each other. I told him I wanted to marry his daughter and wanted his permission to do so.

For a while he didn't say anything. Then he asked, "How do plan to take care of her while you're going to school."

I dreaded this question but knew it was coming. He was probably thinking that a man is supposed to take care of his wife. Until he could do so, the idea of marriage should wait. Nat and I didn't want to wait three more years so I took a deep breath and told him the truth.

I could take care of myself and pay for my schooling, but Nat would have to work to take care of herself.

I waited knowing her father was very old fashioned and would frown on a man who couldn't provide for his wife. To my surprise, he said, "If you two have worked it out, take her."

Christmas Eve, I gave Nat a marquis diamond engagement ring and asked her to marry me. Nat accepted my proposal and we were both ecstatic over the prospect of marriage.

Nat was devastated when I had to leave for Tuskegee. She told me she never wanted us to be separated again.

I told her everything would be all right. Once we were back to our school routines, time would pass swiftly.

I don't know what happened next. I assume Nat and her mother made some decisions without consulting me. The next thing I knew, Nat was sending me a sample of a wedding announcement for a double wedding to be held that coming summer between Nat's sister, her fiancé and Natalie and me. I had planned to marry her anyway but not this soon.

I decided to go along with the program. This would not be the last time Nat's mother over stepped her bounds with Nat and me. It caused a strained relationship through out my early marriage.

When I accepted the fact that I was going to get married that summer, I talked to the chairman of Tuskegee's math department about the possibility of a job for Natalie the following fall.

He was polite but didn't really seem interested.

I showed up at his office so often that he told his secretary to stop making appointments for me.

Realizing I wasn't making any headway, I called my mother (who was now Dean Of Admissions at NCC) and asked her to send me Nat's transcript.

She did and I carried it to the chairman's office. When the secretary saw me, she started to make some excuse but I told her I just wanted to drop Natalie's transcript off.

I left and made a few stops before I returned to my dorm. By the time I reached the dorm, the chairman of the math department had called me three times. He wanted to know how to get in touch with Natalie and wanted to send her a contract.

I was doing janitorial work for spending money. I had student loans to pay for my education. I was secure with what I needed but I couldn't take care of a wife. With this job for Nat, our money worries were over.

After completing the first year of veterinary school, I went back to Durham for the summer and took a job on an assembly line for IBM making keyboards for computers. The job paid well and I needed the money to pay for my next semester's schooling.

One of the young white men on our assembly line took great pleasure in teasing me about my education. He said, "You have all of that education and you're in here doing the same job as me, a high school drop out". He didn't realize that at the end of the summer, I would be gone but he would still be there. The assembly line workers worked at a leisurely pace.

How many parts you could put together in a day set the production limit. If you met production, everything was good. You were paid well and had security. I learned that if production numbers were increased on a position for two weeks, that new number would then become the new production limit.

If you could not make production, you may get a reduction in your salary, moved to another position or fired.

I found out that the man who had harassed me all summer was going to take the position I was in when I left at the end of the summer.

Three weeks before I was to leave ,I began picking up the pace on my position. Before long I had tripled production at my position and was able to hold it there for two weeks. I was careful to maintain the same high standards expected in the job. I didn't take breaks and only stopped ten minutes to eat. It was extremely difficult to work at that level.

I don't know what happened to the guy who took my place. I do know no one could work at that level for any length of time. I imagine he remembered me every morning when he punched in his time card -at least for awhile.

The wedding was planned for mid summer in Durham. Everyone wanted to come. It was a double wedding and most people had never attended such a thing. The wedding was fantastic.

I was in a trance and can't remember details. Dad came from California. Leon, my brother, was my best man. Everything turned out well. I was so nervous that I put on my brother's tux. I was heavier than Leon so the tux I put on was very tight while his hung off of him.

Nat was wearing a beautiful gown. Later I learned the zipper broke while Nat's mother was zipping her up. So her mother sewed the gown on her.

Nat and I spent three days in the honeymoon suite of one of Durham's fancier hotels and then I went back to work for IBM.

We moved in with my mother for the rest of the summer. Mom gave us her bedroom. She moved back to the back porch bedroom to give us privacy. It seems that Mom was always giving up her bedroom.

BOO! I Scared You

Nat and I moved to Tuskegee and into the Married Students Apartments. This was to be our home for the next three years. The apartments were singled story with two bedrooms, one bath, a living room , and kitchen.

The apartments were furnished but nothing matched. We had an orange sofa and two white chairs. Two of the three living room walls were pink and the third was a dark blue.

I asked the management if we could decorate the apartment with furniture we purchase and repaint the walls. The management had never had such a request but allowed us to do this. We made our apartment beautiful and soon other tenants were copying our lead.

I quickly learned Nat was a creature of habits. I am a practical joker and took advantage of her predictable ways.

Nat left for work each morning in her Oldsmobile at 8:30 am for her 9 am class. I left at 7:30 am on my motorcycle for my 8:00 am class.

Nat would get home at 3:30 pm, go straight to our bedroom, open her side of our double closet (with sliding doors), remove her house coat ,and change out of her work clothes.

One day I got home earlier than usual and decided to play a joke on her. I parked my motorcycle in front of our apartment door. Nat parks in the parking lot.

When I saw her drive up, I cut off all of the apartment lights and slipped into her side of the closet.

Nat opened the apartment door without noticing my motorcycle. She came into the bedroom humming a song and I strained to keep from giggling. She came to the closet and tried to slide her side of the door open. I was holding it closed from the inside. It never dawned on her that there was no latch or anything else to keep the door from opening. She stopped trying and started removing her dress, still humming. I released my grip on the door to cover my mouth to stifle a giggle.

Just at that moment she tried the door again. The door opened about three inches before I slammed it closed again.

She now realized someone was in the closet. She was very quiet and I could hear her breathing. Eventually she said, "George, please tell me that's you in there". I stepped out and she was too relieved to be mad at me.

A few weeks passed since my great practical joke. I came home noticing her car in the parking lot. When I reached the apartment door, the apartment was dark.

Just as I was opening the door, the Orkin man(pest control) asked if he could come in and spray my apartment,

I said sure, knowing my wife was hiding somewhere in the apartment. He sprayed the kitchen, the living room and started toward the bedrooms.

He opened the bathroom and Nat jumped out. They both just stood there until I said, "That's my wife, she likes to hide from me."

 Nat was pretty embarrassed but at least she had her clothes on.

For the next three years, every time I crossed paths with the Orkin man , he would stop me and ask, "Does your wife still hide from you in the bathroom?"

I would smile and answer, "Every now and then."

Fred, The Genius Next Door

Fred was our next door neighbor. He was from Texas. His family was well off. He was some sort of genius. Computers were new to everyone. Fred set up the computer system all over campus and was the man to call if anyone had a problem.

He had been a student at Tuskegee for six years and wasn't close to graduating. He would sign up for a class, get bored with the class and drop it. He knew more than most of the professors. His parents paid the bill so the school tolerated him.

It was hard to hold a conversation with Fred. One day as I was leaving the apartment for class, I ran into Fred as we were heading for the parking lot. I said, "Sure is humid".

Fred engaged me for a half hour talking about the differences between actual and relative humidity. I was late for class that day.

Nat and I wanted to get a window air conditioner for the apartment. The outlets were 110 volts so the largest unit that could run on the outlets was a 10,000 BTU. I asked Fred about it.

He said I should get a 20,000 BTU unit like he had in his apartment. He said he rewired his apartment and would be happy to rewire mine. He let me in his apartment to show me how he had done this. Wires were running everywhere. Fred really didn't care how things looked, only if it worked. I told him, "I think we will stick with the smaller unit."

Fred was waiting at my door when I came home that afternoon. He had several pages of computer print outs showing why the larger unit was better and more efficient than the smaller unit. I told him I would read over it. Nat and I still chose the smaller unit.

One weekend, Fred knocked on my door. He asked if he could come in and measure the voltage on my refrigerator. I said, "Sure."

Fred had some sort of voltage meter with him. He went over to the refrigerator and took measurements (I assume of voltage) and wrote some stuff down. He thanked me and was on to the next neighbor's house.

A few weeks later, an engineer from the university was at our door with a distinguished man from Amana Appliances. They were looking for Fred. I told them Fred usually arrived around this time but I hadn't seen him yet. They asked to come in and I obliged them.

The stranger asked if we had any problems with our refrigerator. We said no. He looked it over and opened the door. When he opened the freezer compartment, he asked how often we defrosted. Nat told him at least twice per month or it would cake up with ice regardless of the setting.

He grumbled and wrote something down. The man from Amana told us Fred had written a letter to Amana complaining about voltage leaks in certain of our refrigerators. He had been sent down to check on the problem.

He asked us what we knew of Fred. I told him Fred was extremely intelligent. At that moment, Fred was walking past our door on his way to his apartment .I called to him and he came in. I introduced him.

The man from Amana immediately tried to intimidate Fred by asking him questions in a rather harsh manner. Fred was not bothered by the aggressive nature of the man from Amana.

Fred excused himself and went next door to get his voltmeter. He took measurements all over my refrigerator as he talked with the Amana representative.

Fred explained that there was definitely a voltage leak and this particular refrigerator was nowhere near the worse.

The Amana man shook his head and said the leak didn't represent a problem.

Fred reached for our food blender, unplugged it and set it on top of the refrigerator. He switched it on and it ran. It ran as if he had it plugged in.

This got every one's attention. Fred explained if someone touched the refrigerator while they had their hands in water, they could receive a severe shock.

The Amana man was now nervous. He asked for the model number of the refrigerator. Fred without hesitation or referring to notes replied, "Its an Amana 783QDY. The Amana man smiled and said, "That's the floor model number. I need the model number from the back of the refrigerator". Without hesitation and again without referring to notes, Fred said, "YDJ45L338M43z1880095".

The Amana man's jaw dropped. He was now as impressed with Fred as all who knew him. A month later, everyone in the apartment complex had a brand new Amana refrigerator.

Large Animal Medicine

In veterinary medicine school, we had many courses such as biochemistry, microbiology, feeds and feeding, physiology, etc. that were required but didn't require handling animals.

Our toughest course my freshman year was anatomy. It carried 7 credit hours. We studied the dog for an entire semester. In our second semester we covered cats, horses, cows , and pigs. Once we understood the dog in detail, the rest of the animals were easy. We only had to concentrate on the differences.

We had limited contact with live animals during our first two years of veterinary medicine. There was one exception. Our physiology course required us to have some contact with frogs, mice, and rats.

In our final two years, we had clinical courses and handled all kind of animals.

I took a fancy to large animal medicine (farm animals) probably because I had never been on a real farm and the big animals fascinated me.

My class had been reduced to 28 students by our junior year. We rotated in groups of three (three juniors, paired with three seniors) through several stations of medicine throughout our junior and senior years.

My favorite station was ambulatory. That's when we would get a call from a farmer and have to ride out to the farm and treat an animal on their premises. Most of the students hated ambulatory because most calls came in at night. We had to get to the school's designated parking area, get in the ambulatory truck and head out to a farm. We were instructed by the doctor on call as to what the particular call was about and quizzed on how we would personally handle it.

When I wasn't on ambulatory rotation, I would leave my name on the board so if a call came in after hours and there was room on the truck, I could go. Even when they didn't have room, I would follow them on my motorcycle.

I was constantly in our school's holding areas for large animals and small animal clinics, studying the cases that were there. I could read about a case from a textbook all day and not retain the knowledge. Once I saw a condition, I never forgot it. I can truthfully say, no case ever came through the large and small animal clinics and stayed over night without my seeing it (if I was in town).

One evening I was on the ambulatory truck with an Instructor and four other students. We had to castrate about 50 piglets at a farm.

Before we could get started, we received another call from a farmer whose cow was in heavy labor and needed immediate help.

As our instructor prepared to leave, the pig farmer screamed, "What about me! I called you first and I've gathered up all these piglets. You need to finish here before you leave".

The instructor was in a dilemma. He decided to leave a few students with the pig farmer and the rest would go with him to the calving. The problem was everyone wanted to go to the calving.

He left me with a scalpel, a 5cc syringe, a 16-gauge needle, a bottle of penicillin, and a bottle of iodine. I was to castrate the piglets, give them an injection of penicillin, and douse the wound with iodine.

The instructor and students left. The pig farmer and I got to work. He would grab the first piglet by its hind legs and hold it over the fence. Now it was time for me to do my stuff. Doing this procedure correctly, there is little to no blood. The skin is incised over each testicle causing very little bleeding. The testicles pop up into the incision and I grasped one at a time and pulled with continuing pressure until they popped out of the piglet. This pulling stretches and thins the testicle's arteries and veins until they break. There is no bleeding with this procedure. After about the tenth piglet, we had our rhythm going. We were getting faster and faster.

Then disaster struck. As I made an incision, the intestines spilled out of the opening. This was a scrotal hernia. This would be easy to fix with the proper instruments, but they were all on the truck with the instructor.

The pig farmer was gracious. He said, "We might as well just hit this one in the head to keep it from suffering."

I said, "Wait a minute. Let me think?"

I came up with a plan out of sheer desperation. I pulled a button from my shirt and untangled the thread that held it on. I pushed the intestines back through the incision. I stuck the needle from the syringe through the skin on either side of my incision and stuck the thread through the needle. I pulled the needle out and tied off the thread. I continued pulling buttons and using thread until the piglet was completely sewn up. .

We continued to castrate piglets at a slower pace not wanting to make the same mistake twice.

When the instructor returned, I was leaning against the fence as the pig farmer exalted my cleverness. The instructor took everything in stride and didn't say a word until we were all back in the truck and heading back to school.

Then he said, "I've only got one thing to say about this situation. Any fourth year student that can't recognize a scrotal hernia before he cuts is going to make one sorry vet."

I rode back to school in silence. My ego and confidence were shattered.

Another time I was strolling through the stables at school and saw a large number of students gathered around one of the back stalls.

A farmer had brought his horse to the clinic. He said he thought something was caught in its throat. It kept its neck stretched out and was drooling heavily.

The farmer said the horse hadn't eaten or drunk anything in several days. He had tried to stick his hand in the horse's mouth to see if he could feel anything caught in its throat but found nothing.

Several of the students tried their luck reaching in the horse's mouth as they waited for an instructor but to no avail. I watched for a few minutes and then a horrible thought came to mind.

I looked closely at the farmer's hands and he had cuts all over his hands and forearms. I looked at the horse's legs and saw many wounds that could have been bite marks. None of the veterinary students was wearing gloves during their examination of the horse. I asked,"Has anyone considered rabies?" A hush came over the students. Everyone who had touched the horse started washing and disinfecting their hands. One of the students rushed off to get an instructor.

The instructor's initial exam determined rabies was certainly a possibility. He explained the condition to the owner. Rabies is 100% fatal if untreated before the symptoms develop. The only way to diagnose the disease is to euthanize the horse and send its head to a laboratory with the ability to run a test on the brain.

The now frightened farmer gave the instructor permission to proceed with the test. One week after the horse head had been sent to the lab, the results came back.

The horse was positive for rabies. Everyone who had handled the horse had to undergo rabies treatment. This consisted of a series of very painful injections in the abdomen over a couple of weeks.

From that point on, students were not allowed the freedom of examining animals without an instructor's presence.

Russell's Plantation

Russell's Plantation was a 162-acre farm owned by Tuskegee University. It was a far piece from the school. It had been left untouched for many years and was a hunter's paradise.

The plantation house was no longer there ,but a huge barn behind the site of the old house was still there.

Fraternities like to take their pledgees to this old barn. They always carried them there in the dead of night. They took them up to the hayloft and told them ghost stories most of the night. Then they left the pledgees to spend the remaining night in the loft.

The loft had huge double doors that were always open. Unbeknownst to the pledgees, a giant barn owl lived in the loft. At night he would fly out of the door and hunt all night. At first light, he would fly into the loft through the large open doors.

The owl was always gone when the pledgees entered the loft. The frat brothers knew the pledgees would have had a restless night after hearing so many ghost stories. They would finally be in a deep sleep when the giant owl returned.

The frat brothers would be hiding outside of the barn waiting for all hell to break loose early the next morning as the owl re-entered the loft. One pledgee told of being awakened by the sound he had never heard. It went "wooosh- wooosh" in a slow rhythmic manner. He peered through his droopy eyelids and saw this huge bird whose wingspan filled the entire open doors of the loft. His screams woke the other pledgees and they all vacated the loft screaming in fear. They were greeted by the fraternity brothers who were hysterical with laughter and were carried back to campus.

(Scaredy Cat)

Wayne was one of those guys who wanted to fit in with the regular guys. He was just a little odd and never quite made the cut.

One day a group of the male vet students decided to go to Russell's Plantation to hunt deer. Some had rifles. Others had shotguns. Wayne had never been hunting and was ecstatic that he had been asked to come.

In expectation of his first hunting trip, Wayne had bought a complete hunting outfit including a vest, pants, boots, a hat, and jacket. He had also purchased a shotgun, 306 and a 30/30 rifle.

We arrived at the plantation at 4 am, parked our cars, and started walking down a dirt road to reach a suitable hunting area. A squirrel barked at us from a nearby tree. Wayne grabbed one of his rifles and was trying to site the creature making that awful noise. Several of us had to duck when he swung the rifle in our direction.

We realized Wayne could be a danger to the rest of us if we didn't take special precautions. We gave Wayne the first spot. It was just on a little rise that overlooked the road. We told Wayne to stay in that spot and don't shoot at anything that wasn't on that road. The rest of us were going deeper into the woods. We all had whistles. The plan was we would blow our whistles as we were coming back to the road. No one was to fire once they heard a whistle blowing.

After everyone had been settled for about an hour, we heard shots- lots of them. It sounded like World War Three had started. No one moved. When the shooting finally stopped, we started blowing our whistles and coming out of the woods.

When we reached Wayne, he was shaking. Sweat was pouring down his face and he was pale white. All of his guns had been fired. We asked him what had happened. He said a bobcat attacked him. He said he thought he had shot it in the road.

We all went down to the road to investigate. There, lying in the road , was a rabbit. We all fell out laughing. Then one of the guys noticed the rabbit didn't look right. It was covered in a substance that looked like saliva. Further investigation showed a three-foot section of what appeared to be intestines leading up the hill to the place Wayne was stationed. We found more intestines at Wayne's station and followed even more as they went back into the woods. Fifty feet from Wayne's position we found a forty-five pound bob cat.

It had been shot through the abdomen and was now dead.

We pieced the story together and this is what we think happened. Wayne was in position and the bob cat was walking down the road after just killing and eating a rabbit.. Wayne must have made a sound that attracted the cat. (Wayne said the cat was approaching him in a stalking manner). Wayne grabbed his scoped 306 but the scope had fogged up and he couldn't see the cat. He then grabbed his shotgun and fired at the cat. It was hit in the abdomen, which knocked the just eaten rabbit out of its stomach. The cat began spinning and running trying to get away. It wasn't in an attack mode. It was fleeing for its life and just by chance headed straight for Wayne. Wayne jumped to his feet and started firing every weapon he had as the big cat ran past him stripping out pieces of its intestines as it ran.

The hunting trip was over. All of Wayne's gunfire had certainly frightened anything within earshot away. We didn't get a deer but we sure got a good story.

Rick, Jim, And The Snake

I met Jim and Rick in Vet school. They were white and both were from the north. Rick was a real outdoorsman. He wore his hair long and was extremely knowledgeable about wild animals. I fancied myself an outdoorsman, but I was a rank amateur compared to Rick.

Rick had heard Russell's Plantation was overgrown and full of wildlife. We decided to go there snake hunting one night.

I drove. Jim was in the passenger's seat and Rick was sitting behind me. I was carrying several knives. Jim and Rick had knives. Jim had a long barrel revolver that he laid on the seat between us.

When we got out of town and a good ways down a country road, we saw a car, parked on the opposite side of the road, facing us. As I approached it, the driver cut on his flashing lights. It was a police car. I slowed down and he cut off his lights. When I increased speed, he cut them on again. I pulled across from him and stopped.

A white officer got out of his car and approached mine. I hadn't done anything wrong but this was Alabama. He reached my car and asked to see my license and registration. I produced them and he checked them out. He handed them back and turned to leave. Dumb me asked if there had been any trouble.

He returned to my car and said, "There's been a shooting just up the road." At that point he saw the gun lying between Jim and me.

He asked if the gun belonged to me.

Jim answered, "Its mine. I don't have a permit, but it's not concealed."

The officer said, "Hand it to me!"

I lifted the gun by its barrel and handed it out the window. A black officer was still in the patrol car. He saw his partner turn to leave, then turn back to the car and take a large pistol from the car.

He jumped out of the patrol car, pulled his weapon, and had it trained on me. He was shouting, "Get out of the car! Get out of the car"!

I opened the door with my hands held high and tried to explain. He grabbed my arm, threw me across the hood of the car, and began patting me down. He must have found six knives on me.

Jim stepped out of the passenger's side of the car and approached the officer frisking me. He tried to give an explanation and the officer flung him over the hood and frisked him. They never checked Rick and strangely they returned all of my knives to me. They placed Jim under arrest for carrying a gun and put him in the patrol car.

Jim was scared. He begged us to follow them and don't leave him. We were all scared.

The sheriff questioned us and determined we were no threat to anyone , but he was going to keep the gun and charge Jim with possession of a firearm without a license. He let us go and told us we had to appear before Judge Childress in two weeks. He gave us the address and turned us loose. We were no longer in the mood for snake hunting. We went home.

Two weeks passed. Rick, Jim, and I put on shirts and ties and drove out to see Judge Childress. As we approached the address, we passed a filling station. We didn't see anything that resembled a courthouse. The numbers of the houses pass the filling station were greater than the address we were trying to find. We thought we must have missed the courthouse. After three trips in both directions, we decided to stop at the filling station and ask for directions.

As we pulled in, no one came out to greet us. We went inside and the owner was in a dirty office with his feet propped up on his desk. He was watching "I Love Lucy" on a small black and white TV set.

I said, "Excuse me sir. We're trying to find (and I gave the address)."

He replied without ever taking his eyes off of his program, "You've found it."

I said, "We're trying to find Judge Childress."

He replied again without looking away from his program ,"You've found him."

I thought, "Oh Lord, we're going to jail."

Judge Childress was a decent man. He listened to our story while still watching his program and said he would charge us a $50.00 fine and keep the gun.

Jim explained it was a family heirloom and he was given charge of it and could he please get his gun back.

The judge said, "Sure, for another $100.00". Even though Jim was the only one charged, we all chipped in. We were in this together.

The next time we went to Russell's Plantation hunting for snakes, it was during daylight.

We found an old shed and were looking through it. Rick had a mirror on the end of a rod that he used to look on top of beams without having to climb up on something. He spotted our first snake, a four foot long red rat snake. He quickly captured the snake and dropped it in a pillowcase carried by Jim.

We finished searching the shed and went out in a large field. I was getting bored. Why were we in this open field ? Whenever I found snakes, they were always under a piece of wood or in some sort of debris. I walked along and saw a large tractor tire. As I approached it, a huge snake ran out from under my foot. It went over then into the tractor tire. I hollered for Rick. He and Jim came running. I pointed at the tire and managed to say, "Snake."

He asked, "What kind?"

I answered, "Big."

I was pointing to the tractor tire. Without hesitation, Rick grabbed the tire and lifted it. He asked, "Where's the snake?"

I answered, "He went inside the tire."

Rick began to roll the tire. As he did, a loop of the snake's body protruded from the tire. In a moment of insanity, I grabbed the loop. Then I realized that I hadn't identified the snake. I didn't know if it was poisonous or not. I started rapidly pulling the snake out of the tube, realizing again that I didn't know which end would come out. I needed to grab the head to prevent a bite. I pulled and pulled and the snake kept coming. Finally the head appeared and I was able to grab it before it bit me.

It turned out to be a ten-foot long coach whip snake. It was big and beautiful. It was not a native specimen of North Carolina so I had never seen one. Rick immediately knew what it was. It was so named because as it matured, its head and about a foot down its body was black. The rest of the snake was an olive grey. This resembled the handle and body of a whip.

Some southerners called them hoop snakes. An old wives tale said they were known to grab their tails and form a hoop and roll after you. Pure nonsense. This was without a doubt the largest snake I had ever caught. I had a little bit of a swagger as we continued to search the field.

Later I saw Rick kneeling down and swaying his left hand in an odd motion as he made several attempts to grab something with his right hand. As I approached, he warned me to stay back. Now I could hear the distinct high, piercing, unmistakable sound from the vibrating tail of an angry rattlesnake. Rick was waving his left hand in front of the snake making it strike. As the snake struck, Rick would jerk his hand out of the way while trying to grab the rattler behind its head with his right hand. I was paralyzed. I had never seen a more dangerous or foolish act as this. After several attempts, Rick was successful and had my undying respect. The rattler was a five and a half foot Eastern diamond back rattler. He had a very thick body and though shorter than the coach whip snake, outweighed him by quite a bit. It was an impressive specimen.

Eastern Diamond Back Rattler

We ended up with lots of snakes. Rick wanted to teach people that snakes should be respected but not feared. He wanted to do lectures on snakes for the school. He set up one for just veterinary students, One for biology majors and one for the general public. This didn't work. When people found out about these lectures, the place was packed with no regard for whom the lecture was intended. So he resorted to three lectures per year for anyone who wanted to attend.

Rick was the speaker and certainly was extremely knowledgeable. I was the snake handler. When he talked about snakes in general, I would carry one of our more gentle snakes out in the audience to let people touch and sometimes hold a snake.

When Rick reached the point in his lecture that dealt with poisonous snakes, I would bring the rattler on stage in his escape proof cage. Rick would put small squares of tape over the rattler's eyes and turn him loose in the center of the stage. The rattler would immediately go into a coil. He would vigorously vibrate his tail and stick out his forked tongue sensing danger. The audience would usually ooh and ah at the site and sound of the big snake.

I would be off stage filling a balloon with hot water and attaching it to a long pole. Then I would wait for my cue.

Rick was explaining to the audience, "Most of the poisonous snakes in the United States are pit vipers. They have a hole on each side of their face between the eye and the nostril that contained heat detector cells. Pit vipers don't have to see you to know where you are."

That was my cue. The snake was blinded by the tape but could sense the presence of people in front of him. I would walk on stage with my pole and balloon filled with hot water.

Rick would continue his lecture about pit vipers. He would tell of the Indian snake charmers, "The charmer plays a sort of fluted instrument and sways to the sound of the music. As these men play their music, the snakes (cobras) are in a lidded straw basket in front of the snake charmers. As the charmer lifts the lid, the cobra raise up."

That was my second cue. I would hold the pole out so the balloon was near the rattler. Rick would continue, "The snake will appear to sway with the music." I would then move the balloon around the snake in a rhythmic manner. The rattler would follow the balloon wherever it went. Rick would say, "The truth is, snakes can't hear. The snake is on guard, following the movement of the charmer."

The charmer must continue to sway as he closes the lid on the basket to secure the snake. At that moment I would stop the movement of the balloon. The rattler would strike out, hitting the balloon with its sharp fangs. The balloon would make a loud pop. Water would go flying and many people in the audience would scream.

Rick would end the show by milking the rattler (extracting venom from the poison glands). He sold the venom to hospitals for research and medicine. He then took questions and there were always hundreds of questions.

After one of these lectures, I saw that Rick's hand was severely swollen. I asked him what had happened. He said the rattler had been so angry that he bit through his lower lip. As he put the snake back in its cage, a fang had scrapped his hand.

I was horrified, "Why didn't you say something. We need to get you to the hospital."

Rick said, "I just spent two hours telling people they shouldn't be afraid of snakes. If you had rushed me out of here, the whole talk would have been in vain."

In the many lectures Rick performed in those years of veterinary school, the rattler never failed to strike at the appropriate time and never missed the balloon and the audience never failed to scream.

One summer Rick and Jim were going back North. They had made arrangements with the Dean of biology to keep the snakes in the Biology building. The dean agreed to keep all but the rattler.

They asked if I would keep the rattler. I said, "Sure". The rattler was in a cage designed by Rick. It was an excellent cage. There was no way of escape and was designed to protect the snake from self- damage as he sought a way to escape.

I carried the rattler home and put the cage in the small second bedroom of our apartment.

When Nat got home from work, I warned her not to go into the small bedroom. She made a beeline for that room. As soon as she opened the door, the rattler sounded off. She was terrified. I explained the situation and told her I was the only one that would keep the big snake.

Nat never went to the back rooms unless I was with her. She would not go into the apartment if I wasn't home. This lasted two weeks until Nat got her paycheck. She packed her bags and said she was going home to Durham and wouldn't come back until the snake was gone.

I begged and pleaded with the Dean of biology to let me keep the rattler with the other snakes. He finally relented after I agreed to come over once per week to clean the cage and feed the snakes.

In order to clean the cage, I had to remove all of the snakes. There was no place to put them except on the floor. The room that housed the snakes was designed to house reptiles. There were no places for the snakes to hide. The room was designed with no closets, shelves or crawl spaces.

There were two poisonous snakes in our collection, the rattler and a water moccasin. I wasn't concerned about the rattler. I had handled him plenty. The moccasin was another story. He was mean, aggressive and a ground stander (most snakes want to hide from you. The moccasin wouldn't hide. He would stand his ground and strike as long as you're within reach). I needed another person in the room with me when I cleaned the cage. I didn't need help in handling the snakes. I needed a second set of eyes to watch the snakes, especially the moccasin so I didn't step on them forcing them to defend themselves.

The dean wanted to watch me handle the snakes so he agreed to work with me. that first week. He stayed in a corner by the door as I worked. I didn't talk to him. I was concentrating too hard on what I was doing. When I had removed all of the snakes and had cleaned the cage, I asked him if it was safe for me to step back. He didn't answer. Thinking he hadn't heard me, I asked again. When he still didn't answer. I slowly turned being careful not to lift my feet. The dean was in the corner with his face to the wall crying softly and too terrified to move or speak.

 I tried to assure him that everything was all right. I located the moccasin and put him in the cage first. The rattler was next. As I scooped up the nonpoisonous snakes , some would slither across his shoes, causing a pitiful whimper to escape his lips.

Once everything was in its cage and I told him it was safe to open the door, he was gone. He never looked back. He never said a word. He just left. He avoided me the rest of the summer. He refused to see me even when I stopped by to thank him at the end of the summer. I guess he was embarrassed. I never said anything to anyone about this. I appreciated the fact that he allowed me to keep the snakes in that room.

My "Honda Dream Motorcycle"

Honda made a motorcycle that was nicknamed "The Poor Man's Harley". It was a bulky road bike with a windshield and fiberglass saddlebags as standard equipment. It only had a 300cc engine compared to Harley Davidson's 1200cc engine. It would top end at 60mph. It was impressive to look at but very poor in performance.

Nonetheless, I loved that old bike. I enjoyed getting up early Sunday mornings, putting on some nice clothes, hopping on my Honda, and heading out to the Interstate. While riding, other bike riders would join me. We didn't know each other but were comrades for the moment. It wasn't unusual to wind up with15 or more bikers just riding to ride.

My Honda had a large plastic adjustment knob in the middle of my handlebars. When I was on a highway, I would tighten the adjustment until the handlebars locked. This prevented sharp or sudden turns. You turned the bike by leaning left or right for a smooth, slow turn. This adjustment was ideal for open road travel. I loosened the adjustment when I was on narrow roads or roads that required a sharp left or right turn. This loose setting was necessary for in-town driving.

One Sunday morning while returning to my apartment after a brisk ride on the Interstate, I decided to take the back roads home. I was looking forward to riding on "Black Snake Road". This was a particularly winding road that had been pitched in the wrong direction. Roads are pitched so that the inner part of a curve is lower that the outer part of the curve. Vehicles hug the road better when roads are pitched correctly. Black Snake Road had been pitched wrong and drivers could easily loose control of their vehicles when rounding the curves of this winding road.

I was fresh off the highway and onto Black Snake Road. Traffic was nonexistent so I was moving along at a good clip. I entered the first turn and was well into it when I realized I hadn't loosened the handlebar adjustment. The front wheels were locked so the only way to turn the motorcycle was by leaning in the direction I wanted to turn. The turn would be a slow and wide.

I quickly analyzed the situation. The curve was a sharp turn to the right. I could stay on the road but would venture into the on coming traffic lane. Since it was Sunday and traffic was nonexistent, I decided to take a chance. I accelerated to quickly get through that first turn. As I neared the apex of the turn, I saw a car approaching fast. I couldn't stop. My choice was to hit the car head on or widen my turn and go off the road, wide of the oncoming traffic lane.

My best chance was to run off the road. That wasn't going to be easy. The outside of the curve had a six-foot drop off the side of the road. I had no choice. My plan was to run off the road, and as the bike approached the drop off, I would stand up let the bike go between my legs and over the drop. I was hoping to remain safe on the roadside.

Good plan but I had forgotten one important fact. The motorcycle had saddlebags. The incident went as planed. I went off the road, stood up to let the motorcycle continue off the drop and then disaster. The saddlebags caught my legs and over the drop I went. I had let go of the handlebars and with the thrust of the motorcycle, I was lying on my back as the motorcycle went air-born over the drop.

Everything seemed to happen in slow motion. I heard this strange careening sound. I wondered what was making this irritating sound and before I hit the bottom of the drop off, realized I was making this noise. It wasn't a scream or a groan. I can't describe it and I've never been able to duplicate it. It was there and coming from my mouth until I hit bottom.

All of the wind was knocked out of me. My legs were straddling the seat so my testicles were knocked inside of my body. The spokes on the wheels of the motorcycle were bent and twisted. The rims of my back tire were bent out of shape. Through some miracle, the bike had stayed up right. Considering the gravity of the incident, the bike came out pretty good.

I, on the other hand ,was totally traumatized. I was stunned, my back was damaged and most importantly, my testicles were inside of my body. I unzipped my pants and began pressing in a downward motion on my lower abdomen. I was frantically trying to force my testicles back into my scrotal sack.

I was feverishly applying this kneading procedure when the lady driver of the car made her way down the embankment and approached me to see if I was all right. There I was, unaware of her presence ,with my pants unzipped and my hands thrust down my pants pushing and prodding in a feverish attempt to realign my testicles.

Lord only knows what she thought I was doing. She said, "Oh! I guess you're alright". She turned and made her way back up the hill.

I was sore for a while and still have a bad back. I now have three kids. So I guess all is good. I never forgot to change the adjustment on my motorcycle again.

Henderson, Cameron, and Carter

Henderson was my freshman roommate. Carter and Cameron were married when they entered veterinary school. I married after my freshman year and Henderson married before our senior year.

At the writing of this book (44 years after graduation), all of us are still married to those same ladies. The four of us were the only Black men in our senior class.

Our senior year was either easier than the previous years or we had become so accustomed to the endless classes and work that we had acclimated. We enjoyed each other's company. We studied together during the week and spent our weekends playing double deck pinochle at each other's homes.

During these card games, Henderson and I were always partners and Carter and Cameron were partners. The games were highly competitive and you had to have thick skin. We talked a lot of trash. We never kept up with the score but knew how far ahead one team was to the other.

At the end of our senior year, the game was tied. We vowed to come back to our 20th year class reunion and play a final game for the "Pinochle Championship of the World".

We all came back, even Carter who was in Germany at the time of the reunion. No one had played pinochle in 20 years, so we let the game stand in a tie.

PART FOUR
LONG ROAD TO GASTONIA

A Change of Plan

In December of my senior year in veterinary school, I had an accident that changed my future plans. I planned to join the Air Force after graduation so Nat and I could visit some foreign countries before we settled down in the US.

One week before our Christmas vacation, I was working with a bull in an outside stall at the large animal area of the school. When I finished the bull's treatment, I arranged the gates to send the bull back to his inside stall inside the animal housing area.

A junior student was working with me. I told him to get the bull back to his stall while I wrote up the case. The junior was overly anxious to finish for the day so he tried to close the final gate to the housing area's stall before the bull was completely in.

When the gate touched the back leg of the bull, he kicked back, knocking the gate wide open and the bull was loose. The bull ran out of the barn and into the pastures.

The junior told me what had happened. The school had three adjoining pastures divided by fences and each had a gate. The bull was heading for the first gate and I needed to stop him before he got too deep in the pastures.

I jumped on my Honda Dream motorcycle and tried to head the bull off before he reached the first gate. Unfortunately, the sound of the motorcycle spooked the bull and he ran even faster towards the gate. My motorcycle was strictly a road vehicle and wasn't made for off road conditions. I accelerated trying to pass the bull. I was watching the bull rather than where I was going.

When I finally looked forward, I was approaching a narrow ditch at an alarming speed. Unable to stop at speed I was going, I braced for impact. The front wheel of the motorcycle dipped down into the ditch throwing me over the handlebars onto the ground. Before I could react to the crash, the bike flipped high into the air. Fortunately for me, it landed on my right leg, half way between my knee and ankle. I say fortunately because it could have landed on my back or head with devastating results.

I could feel the bones in my leg snap. I reached up and cut the motorcycle off and laid back in semi-shock.

The junior student witnessed the accident and rushed to my side. He asked if I was all right.

I said, "No, my leg is broken".

He asked if I thought I could walk if he helped me. Again I said, "No, my leg is broken. Go get help".

He rushed back to the school and reported the accident. An ambulance was called. Word of the accident went out quickly among the veterinary students and everyone came running.

Veterinary students, voicing their opinions about what to do, surrounded me. My leg was lying at an awkward angle. Some of the students wanted to grab my leg, stretch it, and make a splint to immobilize the break.

I warned them, "If you touch my leg, there would be hell to pay! I mean it! Don't touch me"!

Tuskegee had its own student hospital on campus and it was directly across from the veterinary hospital. It shouldn't have taken very long for an ambulance to reach me. Dr. Adams (a professor at the vet school and head of the Large Animal Department at the school) went across the street to the student hospital to find out why it was taking so long to get an ambulance to the accident site. He was told all of the drivers were out to lunch. He grabbed a key from the keyboard, commandeered one of the ambulances, and drove it to the pasture to get me.

Dr. Higgins at the hospital was a gruff old doctor that for some reason had no sympathy for students. He examined me and had my pant leg cut so he could assess the injury. He had a nurse prep my leg as he put on a cap, gown, and gloves. Then to my horror and without the aid of anesthesia or any medication to dull my senses , he set the bones in my leg. He literally stretched my leg out until the muscles fatigued and the bones aligned. He then applied a plaster cast.

It was the worst pain I've ever experienced. My leg was in traction. Any movement of my leg sent pain from the break to my brain. The pain was almost unbearable. Sometimes when I was sleeping, I would dream I was falling and jerk causing that pain to navigate throughout my body.

While in the hospital, the doctor was merciless. Each day my doctor would come into my room and ask how I was doing. I would say my leg hurt a lot. He would lift my cast leg out of its sling and let it drop back to the bed, sending the pain through out my body. He had to know how much pain he was causing me.

He would say, "Well, it's suppose to hurt".

I refused to flinch. I refused to let him see me in pain.

Three days after my accident, I was released from the hospital. The doctor informed me that my leg would heal, but I would walk with a limp for the rest of my life.

School was out for the Christmas holidays. I made the seven hour trip to my mother's home in Durham with great difficulty. The junior student that had been with me when I was working on the bull drove Natalie and me to Durham. I was very grateful for his generosity. I couldn't find any comfortable position on that long ride.

When I reached the front door of my mother's house, she said, "Lord, I thought these days were over".

The next few weeks I was healing but I was still in a lot of pain. When I returned to Tuskegee, I felt I was having more pain than normal.

One night two of my friends and I snuck into the small animal radiograph room and X-rayed my leg. When we developed the X-ray, I broke into tears. The bones were not aligned and not healing.

In animals, the bones have to be perfectly aligned or animals may do damage to the painful limb. They may even chew it off. We align bones in animals far better than this doctor aligned my bones. My friends asked what did I want to do.

I said, "Fix it".

We got a bottled of liquor and some casting material. I drank a good bit but couldn't pass out. We cut off the old cast and my friends stretched my leg to re-align the bones. Then one of my friends recast my leg while the other applied traction.

Over the next three weeks, they re-aligned and re-cast my leg one more time. The pain completely subsided. I was able to continue with my student activities as well as the other students. I was over one crisis but was now facing another. Now my greatest concern was the future I had hoped for with the Air Force.

Plan "B"

During spring break, Nat and I went to California to visit my father. I was still in a cast and hoped to take the physical for the Air Force while in California. My father was a Lt. Col. and I felt his connections might get me pass the physical.

The day of the physical came. Veterinarians enter the Air Force as captains. Even though I had not graduated, I was treated with privilege. I was moved to the front of the line at every station during the long examination period. I went through all of the tests with flying colors and was feeling confident until I reached the final stage.

The medical doctor was my last stop. He looked at me and then at my cast. He called me aside and said, "Son when you get back in line and I call your name, you should take a step back. If I continue this exam, I will classify you 4-F. This will mean you are unfit for the service. It may even affect your ability to get insurance later in life. Since you are here voluntarily and not called to report, you have the option to step back and refuse to continue this examination. I strongly advise you to implement that option."

I objected and gave him a letter from my doctor stating I should recover without complications.

The doctor said, "I don't care what your doctor wrote. I will base this report on what I observe and you will be classified 4-F." When I reached the point at the end of the examination and my name was called, I stepped back and my plans for joining the Air Force were gone. I returned to Tuskegee. The last month that I was in a cast, I didn't need crutches or any other type of support to walk.

When I went back to the doctor to have my cast removed, he asked, "Where are your crutches?"

I proudly told him, "I haven't used crutches in the last two weeks."

He said, "You're going to need them today".

He had radiographs taken of my leg and was amazed when he saw the perfect alignment of the bones.

He said, "I never thought your leg would heal this well".

 I just smiled and never told him about the late night adventures with my classmates.

The doctor signed my release and had a resident remove my cast. When the cast was removed, I looked at my leg. It was covered with a dried dead skin. The odor that emanated from my leg was embarrassing, but there was nothing I could do about it. The resident washed the leg as best he could and told me to get in a tub and soak it when I got home. The resident left. I tried to stand, but my healed leg would not support my weight. Being in a cast for months had caused dis-use atrophy. The muscles in my leg were not needed because the cast had supported my weight. The muscles had shrunk and now my leg was about the size of my arm. It took another month to gain enough strength in my leg to support my weight and a year to walk without a limp.

Students of veterinary medicine were older than the other college students. We had college degrees and some had been in the military before entering vet school. Most were married and some had children. Natalie and I decided to start our family during my senior year since I wasn't going to the Air Force and travel. We would lie in bed and daydream about our future. We wanted three children, a boy, a girl and another boy in that order. Our first child was conceived in April of 1971. This meant the baby was conceived while we were in California and I was in a cast.

North Carolina State University and Bryan, our 1st Born

I was very concerned about my future. My wife was pregnant. I was going to graduate in two months and I didn't have a job. I was so sure that I would be accepted into the Air Force that I hadn't applied for any other position.

A month earlier, Tuskegee Veterinary School had received a letter from NC State University seeking an African American veterinarian for a position at their school. Since I was from NC, the letter was given to me. I wasn't interested at the time. It was a "token job".

This was common in those days. This was the early seventies and many schools and business were integrating. State schools and government funded businesses had to aggressively seek minority staff when positions became available. Certain quotas for minority staff had to be reached or there was a danger of losing federal funding.

I hadn't responded to the letter initially but had not discarded it. I had put away it away in the back of a drawer. Now it had my interest. I pulled the letter out and had to iron the wrinkles out of it. I filled it out and anxiously awaited a reply.

Within a week I had a reply from NCSU. They asked me to come to Raleigh for an interview in June. Graduation was in May so my future would be in limbo for a month.

Natalie and I packed a U-Haul and headed to my mother's house in Durham. I never showed Natalie how nervous I was. I was going to take this job if it was offered no matter what the pay.

Two weeks latter, I had the interview with the Dairy Extension Branch at NCSU. I had never been on a dairy farm but I knew a lot about treating cows. The head of Dairy

Extension carried me around and I met all of the people in his department and in the larger department of Animal Science,

The interview ended and I was told that I would be contacted when they reached a decision. I didn't want to wait any longer so I decided to try a bluff.

I told them, " There are only four African Americans graduating from veterinary schools this year. We have been bombarded with offers from all over the country. I have three offers that I have delayed giving a definite answer because North Carolina is my home and I wanted to hear your offer. These other businesses need an answer immediately and I've put them off as long as I dare".

I was sent to a lounge to wait while the people that could make the decision were convened. They met for about forty - five minutes. They offered me a job paying $13,500.00/year. This doesn't sound like much today, but it was the highest salary received by anyone in my class. I was elated.

I rushed back to my mother's home and gave Natalie the good news. We started looking for a house in Raleigh. I wanted a home in a predominately African American neighborhood. This was 1971 and integration was still relatively new.

My wife and soon to be new baby would be home while I worked. Some days I would be out of town with job related responsibilities. I wanted to be accepted by my neighbors instead of tolerated. We found and bought our first home a small, three-bedroom house in Raleigh.

My position was created to add a minority to the staff. I was in the Dairy Extension Section of the Animal Science Department. I was an extension veterinarian. My job was to give continued education to veterinarians and dairymen through out North Carolina.

North Carolina State University had been the first school in the US to hire a minority extension specialist. That was 25 years before they had hired me. That gentleman had an office in Greensboro at NC at A&T University (an African American university) and only came to NCSU for meetings. He was only allowed to work with "colored" farmers and 4-H children.

I was the second person of color hired to work in the extension program at NCSU. I was hired to work in the full capacity of an extension specialist regardless of race. At that time, there were no minority practicing veterinarians in NC and only one African American dairyman.

The truth of the matter was that I was not qualified for my position. I knew very little about the dairy business and the practicing veterinarians in NC knew much more about veterinary medicine than I. I was very bored with my job and hated going to work each morning.

My next-door neighbor worked the third shift at a post office in Raleigh. He was a functional alcoholic. He got drunk every day after work but never went to work drunk and he didn't drive. Neither of us worked on weekends so we began to watch ball games and drink every weekend. My drinking was rapidly becoming a problem.

Natalie went into labor during one of those weekends. She woke me from a drunken fog early one winter Monday morning. I went to the bathroom and ran cold water over my head in an effort to sober up enough to drive her to the hospital. I managed to dress, get her bag and reach the hospital by 8 am. I sat in the waiting room with a few other husbands when the PA system in the waiting room announced; "Dr. Creed, come to the baby viewing station". Everyone looked around trying to see who would get up and go. I just sat there unwilling to acknowledge this disheveled man reeking of alcohol was Dr. Creed. Furthermore I didn't want to be in the presence of my newborn child looking and smelling like I was.

After a long while, I stood up, left the hospital, went home, bathed and shaved. I put on my best suit and returned to the hospital. I went to the window of the viewing room and for the first time saw my newborn son, George Bryan Creed, who we refer to as Bryan to limit the confusion from our first name. Nat was tired but very beautiful. I decided to stop drinking and to get my life under control.

I took a few days off from work to be with my new family. When I returned to work, it was with a new attitude. I asked to meet with the head of Dairy Extension and told him that if I was going to help veterinarians and dairymen in our state, I needed to know what kind of help they needed. I wanted to take a state car and visit the prominent dairy counties throughout North Carolina. I wanted to meet with the local extension agents and visit veterinarians and dairy farms. This was arranged and I spent the next few months on the road, coming home on Fridays and leaving on Mondays. By the end of this period, I had a pretty good idea of the concerns of the dairy industry and the veterinarian's view on working with dairymen.

Dairymen wanted a veterinarian who would come when they called. Their major health concerns were in the area of mastitis (inflammation of the cow's udder) and reproduction (cows needed to calve yearly to be productive milk producers). Veterinarians couldn't justify farm practices. To travel to farms to see one sick animal was not economically productive, when they could stay in their office and see multiple dogs and cats.

Our Dairy Extension Department already had a specialist working with one of the major dairy cow problems. He had a PhD in microbiology and was already working on mastitis

114

problems when I arrived. That left me with reproduction. I read everything I could find on dairy cow reproduction. I attended meetings all over the US. I learned to palpate cows. (a long plastic sleeve is placed over the arm and you reach into the cows rectum and examine the uterus and the ovaries). I became an expert in cattle reproduction in short order. The state owned three dairy herds. They were at my beck and call. I developed proficiency in palpating cows. With my palpation techniques I could not only tell you if a cow was pregnant, I could come pretty close to telling you the date she was bred.

Over the years I developed a program where the veterinarian visited the dairy farm on a monthly basis, palpated cows, discussed feeding, mastitis issues and managed vaccination programs. If a veterinarian had enough herds, he could justify a full time practice devoted to farm animals. I worked with other scientist and specialist at NCSU and helped develop a computer-generated program that measured the reproductive performance in a dairy herd.

I met with dairymen throughout the state and taught them the importance of regular veterinary visits. I trained veterinarians all over NC in this type of practice. I was soon speaking at veterinary and dairy conferences all over the country. The computerized program I helped develop was now being used throughout the United States

Life was good. Nat had taken a job teaching math at St Augustine University in Raleigh. After three years in our first home in Raleigh, we bought a beautiful new home in Durham (about 18 miles from Raleigh).

I worked at NCSU for five years and things had gone very well. I was very comfortable with my position at NCSU, I was married to my childhood sweetheart. I was living in my hometown in a beautiful new home. We had started our

115

family but I was not content. I wanted to practice veterinary medicine and this was not practice. I was getting too comfortable at NCSU and knew that if I didn't leave soon, I would never leave.

My tri-level home in Durham

I used my time at NCSU wisely. I had access to information of all of the dairy farms in NC. I knew how many farms were in each county. I knew how many cows were in each herd. I knew the average milk production of each herd. I even knew the level of schooling in each farm. I was looking for an area that had a good number of high producing cows with the father or son having attended college.

College was important because I couldn't go to an area and just work on sick cows. I needed the owners to understand preventative medicine. I needed an area that would be receptive to a black veterinarian.

A large part of my reproductive farm visits was palpating cows. This required putting on a shoulder length plastic sleeve, reaching into the rectum of a cow and examining the reproductive organs. This was a dirty job but necessary to determine pregnancy in a cow. I had access to the state owned dairies and their records. Over the years, I used these herds to hone my skills in palpation to the point my skills were unmatched.

I preferred to examine cows "blind." By this I mean, I didn't want to know anything about the cow before I examined her. Dairies were breeding cows by artificial insemination. They had records of the exact day a cow was bred. I reached the point that I could detect a pregnancy 30 days after a cow was bred, After palpating the cow, I would tell the dairyman whether or not the cow was pregnant. If she was pregnant, I would tell him the breeding date. I seldom missed by more than two days. I did this in order to establish the dairyman's confidence in my skills. In time, my skills became legendary. I say this because dairy farmers began enhancing my skills far beyond what they really were.

Creating The Legend

When I was invited to a county to give a lecture to dairymen, it was my practice to arrive early in the morning to visit a few of the local dairies before the evening lecture. The farm visits were arranged by the local county agent. I always wanted to visit the dairy farmer that had the most influence over the other dairy farmers in the region. Once I had him in my corner, he would convince the others.

I visited a farm of a prominent dairyman in Buncombe county. The owner was known to have no faith in veterinarians. I was getting ready to examine the first cow . The owner was sitting on a stool holding his breeding records in his lap. He looked at me and said, "Doc, What percent are you going to get right?"

Puzzled, I asked, "What do you mean?"

He said, "Are you going to guess 50%, 60%? What % do you usually get right?"

I told him, "If I say she's pregnant, she's pregnant. So my answer is 100%."

He just shook his head and mumbled, "Yea, right."

I palpated the first cow. As I entered the cow with my right arm, I felt a tremendous amount of heat. I looked at the dairyman. He was studying his records and not paying attention to me. This cow had a fever and the most common cause was mastitis (inflammation of one of the quarters of the cow's udder). While still palpating with my right hand, I reached down to the cow's udder with my left hand. The right front quarter was very hot and hard.

I finished my exam and the dairyman asked, "OK doc, what did you find?"

I said, "This cow is pregnant. She was bred June 10th and she has mastitis in her right front quarter."

The dairyman's mouth dropped open. I had hit the date right on the nose. He exclaimed, "I just treated that cow for mastitis this morning when I milked her."

He was a believer and I decided to have a little fun with him. I said, "It's a heifer calf and it has a ring around its left eye."

Of course, I couldn't tell any of that but the farmer accepted it as the gospel. Eventually he had a cow give birth to a heifer calf with a ring around its left eye. It certainly wasn't the cow I examined. It may have been two or three years later. He proclaimed I told him about it. He told all who would listen about this veterinarian from NCSU with these awesome skills. And the legend began.

Another time a dairy farmer told the tale that I was scheduled to visit his farm. He was breeding a cow as he saw me drive up. To test my skills, he put this cow in with the cows I was to examine. When I reached the recently bred cow and examined her, I supposedly told him the cow was three minutes pregnant.

Of course that wasn't possible but stories like that began to circulate. I did my best to remain humble but in truth enjoyed hearing these tales.

I Told You So

One of NCSU dairy farms raised Jersey cows. This was a much smaller cow than the Holstein that most dairy farmers in NC owned. I was called to the farm because the heifers (cows that had never had a calf), were ready to breed (age 12-18 months) but weren't coming in heat.

I reached the farm and the herdsman had the Jersey heifers captured and ready for my examination. As I examined the heifers, I found out why they weren't coming in heat. They were already pregnant.

When I informed the herdsman, he just laughed. He said, "That's impossible. These heifers have not been bred and have never been around a bull".

I said, "Not only are they pregnant, but some of them are getting ready to have their calves (gestation for a calf is nine months)".

He continued to laugh and dismissed me. By the time I had reached the university campus, the herdsman had called ahead to tell the Animal Science chair about this crazy veterinarian they had hired and who knew nothing about cows.

I took the abusive laughter and looks without comment, knowing my time was coming. A month later, the heifers started calving, lots of them.

How was this possible? The heifers hadn't been bred artificially and hadn't been near a bull. I was called back to the farm. The herdsman greeted me with a newfound respect. His job was on the line. He wanted me to figure out how this had happened.

It had to be a bull. The herdsman said, "There are no bulls on this part of the farm. We remove them when they are six months old".

That was the answer. The Jersey is one of the most fertile animals on the planet. The heifers and bull calves were kept together until they were six months of age and then separated. Some of the bulls and heifers were fertile enough to breed successfully at that young age. As improbable as that may sound, it was the only possible answer.

We initiated the practice of separating the bull calves and heifers when they were weaned from the bottle (6-8wks old) and the problem disappeared.

Deja vu

 A beef cattleman asked the extension service to send an expert out to determine why his cows were not coming in heat. I was sent. This man had spent a small fortune establishing a herd of Santa Gertrudis (cross between a Brahma and a Shorthorn). He had about 300 cows. He had invested in training and obtaining material to artificially breed his cows. They were not coming in heat and I was called to find out why.

I had him gather about 1/3 of his herd into a holding pen with a long chute and a head catcher. I began examining his cows. All of them were pregnant.

"Impossible!", the owner screamed, "I haven't bred them and they've never been around a bull. What kind of clown does the state have working for them?"

He was really angry and didn't believe me at all. As I walked back to my state car, he walked with me complaining the whole time about needing answers that I wasn't supplying. As I was walking, I noticed a pen with a bull in it.

I questioned the cattleman, "I thought you said you didn't have a bull".

He answered, "I never said that. I said the cows have never been around a bull".

I said, "Maybe he gets out."

The cattleman said, " My herdsman would tell me if he got out. What do you think, it gets out, breeds my cows and then gets back in his pen?"

"No" I said, "He would stay out once he got out."

We continued walking towards my car and I saw a farmhand nearby. I called out to him, "Hey!", he looked my way, "How often does the bull get out?"

He answered, "All the time. We just catch him and put him back in his pen."

I didn't even turn to see the cattleman's expression. I just continued to my car, got in and drove back to Raleigh.

In my practice years, I became interested in reproduction of horses. I could detect pregnancy in a cow as early as 30 days but I could detect pregnancy in a horse as early as 18 days. I had several large breeding farms as clients. They never doubted my skills. This one horse breeder was a different story.

I went to a horse farm that boarded five horses for five different owners. I was called out to the farm to vaccinate and deworm all of the horses. While there, I was asked to do a pregnancy exam on Ms. Miller's mare She was pregnant.

A few months later, Ms. Miller called back. The farrier (blacksmith) had been out to shoe her mare. The mare acted up and gave the farrier a hard time. He said, "This mare's in heat."

She told him, "Dr. Creed examined her a month ago and said she's pregnant, So, she couldn't be in heat."

Not appreciating his knowledge of horses challenged, he said, "I don't care what Dr. Creed said. This mare is in heat."

She asked if I would come and recheck the mare. I said sure. Mares will sometimes reabsorb foals. This was much more common in mares than in cows. Since I detected pregnancies at a very early stage in the 11 months gestation, it was quite possible that the foal had been reabsorbed.

I traveled back to the horse farm. It was quite a ways from my home and I was going to do this at no charge. I always went the extra mile to please my clients. I examined Ms. Miller's mare and much to my and Ms. Miller's relief, the mare was still pregnant. She thanked me and offered to pay me for my time but I refused.

Several months passed and the farrier returned to the horse farm. Again he had trouble with Ms. Miller's mare. He told her again, "This mare's in heat."

Ms. Miller told him that she had called me after the last time he had made that statement. I had come out and re-examined the mare and said she was pregnant.

He didn't care. He told her, "I've been around horses more years than Creed's been alive. I'm telling you that mare's in heat."

Ms. Miller called me again and asked me to come and re-check her mare.

I told her I would, but this time I would charge her for a farm visit and an examination. She said that would be fine. I met her on the farm.

She could tell I was agitated and apologized for calling me but she had to know for sure that her mare was pregnant.I examined the mare and she was pregnant and everything was as it should be.

I didn't hear from Ms. Miller until late one cold winter night. Her mare was in labor and she wanted me to assist in her delivery.

I got out of bed, dressed as warmly as I could and drove the long distance to the horse farm. I got out of my truck and headed for the barn.

Ms. Miller was waiting just inside the door and said, "Dr. Creed, I'm sorry to call you out this late."

I couldn't resist a little jab. I answered, "Why didn't you call the farrier?"

Decision Time

In my travels throughout the state, no area was perfect. Statesville area had the most dairies but in my 6½ years at NCCU, I was only invited to speak in that area two times and only ten farms were represented on either visit.

Gaston, Lincoln and Cleveland counties bordered each other. On the many times I was invited to speak at either of these counties, the room was packed. I was also invited to visit the farms and on many occasions I was fed. This area also boasted the highest "father-son "operations with most of the sons having some college education. Gaston county was the largest of the three counties and its largest city, Gastonia, had a black mayor, several black doctors and blacks were serving on the school board. It was a "no brainer" that we were going to move to Gaston county.

It was hard to leave a job I loved, my new home and the security of my position. I was going to an unknown area and my family would be totally dependent on my veterinary and business skills for our financial survival. I had no business skills and had no idea of how a veterinary business was run.

The Lord blessed me with good common sense, good work ethics, fairness and a reasonable amount of people skills. I went to veterinary school to practice veterinary medicine and if I didn't leave NCSU soon, I knew I would never leave. I set my mind to leave and gave myself a deadline. I would open practice in Gaston Co. NC on October 1st 1976, (two years from that decision date).

Bryan was three years old and we were starting to plan for a second child. I took the national and state Boards June 1975. This was to be a dry run. If I didn't pass I could take them again the following year. I scored well on both state and national written sections. Dr. Crow was the board veterinarian chosen to give me the oral part of my exams. Dr. Crow was practicing farm animal medicine in Gaston county, NC. I would be competition to him when I started my practice. This represented a conflict of interest on his part. I found out later he pulled string so he could give me the exam.

Dr. Crow knew I was a dairy specialist so he didn't ask me anything about cows or any other farm animal. He quizzed me on dogs and cats. He fished around until he found out I was unfamiliar with doses of medicine by weight.

He asked me," How many ccs of acepromazine would you give a 35lb dog?"

I told him, " The dose is on the bottle and I can calculate the amount of ccs."

He said, "You ought to know the dose without having to read the label."

All of the other questions he asked were based on knowing the doses of different drugs. I failed the oral exam.

A year later it was time to retake the oral part of my exams. I was ready for dog and cat questions and was now familiar with medicine doses. I had increased the pressure on myself by submitting my resignation to my department chair. I had to pass the test. I only had to take the oral exam.

When I entered the building, a veterinarian acquaintance came up to me and whispered, "Dr. Crow has stated that as long as he is on the Board, you will not pass the test".

When I entered the test room, there sat Dr. Crow. When I voiced an objection to his giving me the test, he smiled and said I would have to take it from him or fail. I got up and left the room.

I found the president of the NC Veterinary Association and told him of my concern. He asked if I would take the orals under Dr. Crow if he personally stayed in the room with me to make sure the test was fair. I agreed. All I wanted was a fair chance.

When I returned with the President. Dr. Crow wanted to know the purpose of this act. The President said he was there as an observer. Dr. Crow stood up and stormed out of the room.

The president asked me, "Are you married?"

I replied, "Yes. Seven years. "

He asked, " Do you have any children?"

I replied, "One boy and one on the way."

He asked, "What do you intended to do in Gaston County?"

I replied; "Open a farm animal veterinary service."

He said, "Well you got all the answers right. Congratulations! You've passed the oral exam."

2nd Child

Nat and I were planning our second child. I had made specific plans. Since our first child had been a boy, this one should be a girl. I read all kinds of books on how to determine the sex of a child during conception. I applied these methods. I was going to open my practice in Gaston County on October 1, 1976. I wanted to go to Gaston County just after my birthday (September 5th) to set up phone systems, advertise and all of the things one needs to do to establish a business. Nat would need to deliver before I left for Gastonia or she would have to stay in Durham where she had the support of both of our mothers and doctors she knew.

· With Nat's first pregnancy, she showed none of the typical things associated with pregnancy. No mourning sickness, no depraved appetite, no swollen ankles, no mood swings, nothing. With this child, all of that was present. My mind hollered different hormones. This is absolutely a girl. Nat went into labor August 24th

I was allowed to go into the delivery room during the delivery. The doctor delivered our child and said, "You've got a strong, healthy BOY"!

I looked down at Nat and said, "Well honey, we'll just have to try again."

She said, "Not tonight, I have a headache."

We named our son Kevin and two weeks later, we left for Gaston County.

I purchased a mobile veterinary truck. It was a Ford 150 cub cab with a fiberglass veterinary unit filling the cargo space. It had lots of drawers and pull out units, refrigeration, hot and cold running water, surgery sterilization and multiple storage area for drugs and instruments.

PART FIVE

Veterinary Stories

Hollow Tail

I was starting a unique practice for these times. Veterinary medicine had redefined itself. The early veterinarians had limited education. Most were farmers that knew a little more than the average farmer about treating sick animals. Many of their techniques were crude. An example of this is "Hollow Tail". The farmer would call the "vet" because he had a cow that wouldn't get up. The "vet" would show the farmer the cow's tail. It looked strangely shorter than normal.

The "vet" would shake the end of the tail and it would wobble loosely. The "vet would pronounce his diagnosis, "Hollow Tail". He would tell the farmer that the bone in the lower part of the tail had dissolved. Without treatment, this condition would progress until the animal was completely paralyzed. The Vet treated the condition by cleaning the underside of the cow's tail and making a four inch cut along the midline of the tail. He would soak a rag in turpentine and tape the rag to the open wound. The cow would immediately jump up.

In truth the bone only comes a third of the way down any cow's tail. The tail is shorter because the switch (Fluff of hair at the end of the tail) will fall out if a cow has a high fever. The incision and turpentine burnt the cow making her get up from pain. I had a farmer call me out to his farm. Before I could get out of the truck, he came up to my window and asked if I had heard of "Hollow Tail".

I answered, "Yes."

He asked if I treated for it.

I answered, "No."

He told me it was no need of my getting out of the truck. I could just keep on going. So I did.

Now, veterinary training reaches far beyond farm animal experience. Students must get a degree in animal science, biology or chemistry before applying to veterinary school. There is a limited number of vet universities so being accepted to one is not a given. When I attended, one student out of 300 applications was accepted. Veterinary training is a four-year program. The average student graduates from college at the age of 22. Four more years of vet school and they are now 26. Some go on to specialize, 2 more years. The student has now invested 8 – 10 years of college and grad school years and a ton of money. Todays veterinarian is highly educated and multi-skilled.

In my practice my wife Nat, had by far the hardest job. She had to deal with cooking the meals, cleaning the apartment, handling the kids, doing the banking, ordering supplies, answering calls with questions she couldn't answer and learning farm terminology that she didn't understand.

Nat learned to write down exactly what the farmer said and let me interpret. Terms such as "Tell doc I've got a cow that can't find her calf".

Nat answered, "I don't think he's going to come and look for a lost calf". What he meant was he had a cow in labor.

Another was, "I have a cow with a hot quarter". The cow had mastitis (inflammation of the mammary gland).

Having a light quarter was limping on one foot.

Shame on me, I enjoyed her frustration with the terminology that came natural to us "farm hands".

Terry

When we moved to Gastonia, we didn't know anyone. We moved into a very nice apartment complex called Georgetown Woods Apartments Our apartment had three bedrooms, a very nice kitchen, living room, dining room, two baths and a small balcony with a storage area.

At this time, my business was called "Farm Animal Veterinary Service". I had a mobile veterinary truck and I went out to the farms to treat animals. I was on the road most of the day and would go out on emergency calls all hours of the night.

Natalie was mostly in our apartment multitasking. During our first few weeks we hadn't seen another African American in our apartment complex. One day as I was returning from work, I saw what I thought was an integrated family leaving their apartment and going to their car. The man was black, the woman looked white and the young girl with them looked to be about the same age as Bryan.

I rushed into our apartment and told Nat to grab the kids and come with me. We rushed out of the house and jumped into our car just as the other couple was leaving the complex. We followed them until they stopped at a gas station. I approached the man as he was fueling his car.

I said, "Excuse me sir. You may think I'm crazy but my wife and I just moved to this area a few weeks ago and you're the first black people we've seen. My name is George and that's my wife Natalie in the car."

He laughed and introduced himself as Terry. He introduced us to his wife Ion (who turned out to be black but with a very light complexion) and their daughter Monique.

They informed us that there were two more black couples in the complex and invited us to their apartment that night to meet the others. We (four couples) were all near the same age and had children the same age. We became fast friends, especially Terry and I.

Terry was a CPA originally from Gaston County. He had attended A&T University in Greensboro and had earned his accounting degree. He began work with a firm in Greensboro, NC.

His father had put all of his five children through college by operating a custodial and garbage business. His garbage truck consisted of a large truck with side panels. The cans had to be manually lifted and dumped into the bed of the truck.

Terry's father became very ill and had to be hospitalized. He asked Terry and another son, Theodore (a local preacher) to keep his business going until he could come back to work. Theodore picked up the garbage Monday through Friday. Terry would come in on Friday evenings and run the business and do the accounting Saturday and Sunday.

Together they bought their father a used truck with hydraulic lifts so he would never have to lift a can again. Unfortunately his father's conditioned worsened and he died in the hospital.

Terry and Theodore had increased their father's business and had a large sum of money invested in the truck. Terry decided to leave the accounting firm in Greensboro and move back to Gastonia to take over his father's business.

Both of us were starting our businesses around the same time. His business was well under way because of his father's hard work but his business had been a one-man business. Terry was educated, well spoken, very personable and had a lot of great ideas to expand the business. He became very successful. In those early days he would ride with me to some of my farm calls and I would ride with him when I wasn't busy.

134

"Don't Let My Cow Out"

One day Terry road to a farm with me. An old white gentleman owned the farm. I'll call him Jim. He had a few cows and a bull. He had called because his "Black Angus" cow was in labor and couldn't have her calf.

Terry and I drove up and Jim carried us out to his barn. The barn was as old as Jim It had two levels. The upper level was used to store hay. The cow was closed up in the lower level, which had a ceiling only 7 feet in height held up by several poles.

Jim warned me that the cow was mean and in an especially bad mood because of the pain she was in from being in labor for so long.

I went into the enclosure with my trusty lasso. The lasso had a metal quick release so the lasso could be removed with a quick snap if an animal was choking. I had Terry and Jim stay outside until I had secured the cow. I lassoed the cow and let her chase me round and round one of the poles until she had snuggled herself tightly against the pole. I quickly made a halter from the lasso and eased the pressure from her neck.

Terry and Jim then joined me as I corrected the calf's position and delivered a healthy Black Angus bull calf.

Jim laughingly said he would name the calf Terry after my dark skinned friend.

Jim asked me how I was going to release the cow. I told Jim and Terry to leave the barn. I then told Terry to stand outside of the door and leave it cracked. I would release the cow and run for the opening. Once I had cleared the opening, he was to shut the door to keep the cow in.

That was the plan. It almost worked. When I saw that Terry was in position behind the cracked door, I released the cow and started running for the door. The cow immediately came after me. I was fast but she was faster. I could feel her gaining. I didn't look back. I focused on that small opening in the door with Terry peering in. I ran as hard and fast as I could. I had on boots. The ground was muddy from lack of sunlight and a leaky roof.

When I was a few steps from the crack in the door, Jim hollered at Terry, "Don't let my cow out".

Terry slammed the door shut forcing me to veer off at a ninety-degree angle.

The cow couldn't stop and ran into the door, knocking it off of its hinges and on top of Terry and out into the pasture she ran.

I told Jim not to worry. When she settled down, she would come back to her calf. He paid me and we left.

I still pick on Terry about that day. I claim that as soon as a white man gave him an order, he forgot about our friendship and my safety and obeyed the order.

The truth of the matter is that if Terry hadn't closed that door forcing me to veer off, the cow would have hit me in the back and crushed me through that doorway. I would have been lucky to survive with injuries. I haven't told Terry to this day how grateful I am that he shut that door. Its much more fun to make him feel guilty.

"Uncle Remus"

I received a call from a Mr. Archie, the owner of an automobile garage in Dallas, NC. Mr. Archie had a beef cow that was down and couldn't get up. The cow was in his pasture, several miles from Dallas in a very rural area. He said it would be easier for me to pick him up at his business and he would ride with me, showing me the way to the cow. I agreed to this and he rode with me to his farm.

We walked a good way into the woods and found the cow. It was in fairly good condition but a little anxious and dehydrated. I made my diagnosis, treated the cow and slapped her on her hips.

After several tries, she was able to rise. I told Mr. Archie that the cow needed water. I asked if there was a creek or stream near by.

He said, "No but an old nigger lives just over the hill. We could get a bucket of water from him".

I cringed inwardly at the sound of the "N" word but didn't show an outward reaction. Because of my skin color and the texture of my hair, he assumed I was white.

Together we walked over the hill to a small two room cabin. I went on the porch and knocked on the door. It was answered by a very tall black man. His skin was the blackest I'd ever seen. It was smooth and without blemish. His hair and beard in contrast were pure white. He was the perfect replica of my image of my childhood storybook character, "Uncle Remus".

I told him we had a cow over in the woods that needed water and wanted to know if he had a bucket we could borrow and a place to get water.

The old man pointed to a bucket on the porch and said; "That's the only bucket I have. I use it to drink, clean and wash with. You can use it but clean it up when you get through".

I thanked him and he went back inside his cabin. I picked up the bucket and walked over to the pump. As I was pumping the water, Mr. Archie said, "You'd better wash that bucket out. No telling what that nigger had in it".

Again I cringed inwardly but showed no outward reaction. I carried the water over the hill to the cow and it drank eagerly. I then carried the bucket back to the cabin and started scrubbing it with extreme care.

Mr. Archie grunted something under his breath that I ignored. I walked over to Mr. Archie and told him the bill was $90.00. Mr. Archie was shocked. This was in the 70's and $90.00 was a lot of money.

He said, "Doc, I know you saved my cow, but that's a lot of money". Without hesitation and with a firm voice, I repeated, "Mr. Archie, the bill is $90.00".

He reluctantly pulled out his wallet and counted out $90.00. I immediately turned and walked up on the porch and knocked on the door. The old black man answered the door and I handed him $45.00.

He protested, "Oh no! You don't owe me anything".

I turned and pointed to Mr. Archie and said, "That white man over there insists that I give you this money".

He said, "Well, alright then. Thank you".

I smiled and said, "No sir. We thank you".

I looked back at Mr. Archie and if looks could kill, I would have surely been dead. He finally realized I was black. His face was red and his fists were clinched. I walked right pass him without speaking to him. I walked back through the woods and to my truck. I got in my truck and left.

To this day, I don't know how Mr. Archie got home. We didn't have cell phones in those days and old "Uncle Remus" didn't have a phone.

Needless to say, Mr. Archie never called me again. When I told Nat what had happened she was frightened. She was afraid he would get his friends and retaliate.

I assured her Mr. Archie would never tell anyone how two black men got the best of him.

Pig Stories

Hog Castration

My very first job in practice was to castrate a pig. Dr. Gene in an adjoining county had a farmer call him to castrate a pig. He told the farmer that he couldn't come but there was a new veterinarian in town and he would come out and do the job. He set up a time and gave the farmer a price without consulting me.

I didn't mind. It was my first official day of work and my very first farm call. I was excited. Dr. Gene told me there would be plenty of help when I reached the farm and the hog farmer would have the 100lb hog captured when I arrived.

I was driving my brand new Ford F150 Super Cab truck with my state of the art Bowie veterinary unit in the cargo space of the truck. This was a fiberglass unit that resembled an "ice cream truck" unit. It had hot and cold running water, refrigeration, storage space for all of the brand new tools of my trade and slots and racks for medication. It was a very impressive unit.

I lit a cigar and headed out to the farm, thinking, "This is what all of that hard work was about. This is what I've dreamed about".

I reached the farm and things started to unravel very fast. The help that was promised turned out to be an 80-year-old man with a stooped back. The hog was closer to 400lbs than 100lbs. The hog was captured all right. It was running loose in a ¾ acre lot. The lot was fenced with hog wire and was filled with deep slippery mud and hog manure.

I put on my calf length boots, slipped on my one piece coveralls and climbed over the fence. I chased that hog until we were both ready to drop. I had my brand new hog catcher

141

(a 4-foot long contraption with a cable noose on one end. The cable threaded through the contraption and fitted to a handle that when pulled, tightened the noose). I needed to slip the noose over the snout of the hog while his mouth was open, work the noose behind the hog's upper tusk (canine teeth), tighten the noose and lock it in place. Then I had to hold the hog still while I inject a sedative into the ear vein of the hog.

I had done this numerous times while a student at the Tuskegee Vet School. We had a wealth of help and it normally took three strong people to accomplish the task. I was alone with an 80 year old stooped over man that couldn't even climb into the pen.

After an hour of chasing the hog, I finally got him cornered between the fence and a tree. I expertly slipped the noose in place. As I pulled the noose tight, the hog swung its head, jerking the apparatus out of my hand. He ran through the pen swinging its head wildly. He eventually reached an area of the pen that had trees. He swung his head one last time, slamming my brand new, first time used, hog catcher into the trunk of one of the trees. It bent into a useless "U" shape.

I sat there in utter amazement. That hog catcher cost $125.00. I was only being paid $35.00 for this job and still hadn't gotten the job done.

I went back to my truck and filled a large syringe with a triple dose of anesthesia. I picked a large bore needle that would allow rapid injection and climbed back into the pen. I cornered the hog with his rear end pointing back to me and swiftly stabbed the needle into the hog's right testicle, rapidly injecting the contents of the syringe.

The hog squealed and flung around to attack but I had jumped clear. The hog ran out of the corner and crossed the pen moving slower and slower. I had retrieved my scalpel and my emasculator (an instrument used to cut and crush the cords of the testicles without causing bleeding). I moved close behind the hog. When he eventually collapsed, I rushed in and immediately removed the testicle that I had injected with the overdose of anesthesia. This prevented the hog from absorbing any more anesthetic.

This worked like a charm. I had lost my new instrument but learned from necessity, a very easy way to castrate a hog. That was the method I used until the day I stopped treating farm animals.

I climbed back into my truck, tired, dirty, and humbled by a hog.

When I entered my apartment, my wife said, "Go clean up. What do you want for dinner"?.

I said, "Anything but pork."

Tetanus

A hog farmer called me out to look at his young male pig. He and a few of his buddies had castrated a bunch of young pigs about a week ago and they had all done well but one. He noticed it had started to stagger a few days ago. Now it was down and couldn't get up at all.

As soon as I saw the pig, I knew what was wrong. The pig's face was drawn back into a morbid grin. He was stiff and lying on his side. Any sudden movement or noise caused it to shake violently. This was a classic case of tetanus.

Even though I knew what it was and its cause (castrating with unclean instruments) I still gave the pig a complete examination. When I finished the exam, I told the owner my diagnosis and how it needed to be treated.

I would give the pig an injection of penicillin that morning and he would need to give it injections twice per day for the next five days. The owner was very nervous about this. He had never given an injection before. He asked if I would come out come out twice per day and do it for him. When I told him that I would have to charge him for each trip, he decided to give it a try. I assured him it was easy. I told him that I would help him with the first injection and he would see how easy it was.

I showed him what to do. I told him, "Hopefully with the treatment, the pig will recover." I also informed him, "Any time you castrate pigs in the future, give a preventative injection of penicillin. In most cases one injection would prevent the disease."

Four days had passed when the hog farmer called me again. He said, "Doc, I need you to come back out and treat this pig. "

I said, "You mean its not any better?"

He said, "Shucks doc. I've been chasing that pig for more than an hour trying to give him his penicillin. I'll pay you what ever it cost to come out here and give him his final shot."

I laughed and told him to put the remaining medicine in his refrigerator. The pig was healed.

Hog in Labor

I was called out to see a hog in labor. This sow weighed over 500lbs and was in a pigsty full of mud and slop.

I gave the pig an anesthetic injection and herded her to the cleanest area in the pen.

When the anesthetic was in full effect I was able to examine the hog. She was full of dead piglets. They had swollen to the point that they couldn't be extracted vaginally. I was going to have to do a C-section (surgically remove the piglets) there in the filthy pen.

The owner and I placed some hay on the ground and used several bales to prop the pig on her back. I prepped the hog's belly for surgery and prepared my instruments. The hog was still in a deep sleep. I had a second dose of anesthesia ready in case the hog began to wake before I was through with the surgery.

The surgery went well. I removed all of the piglets and had sutured the uterus closed. I was starting to close the body cavity when the hog went from deep sleep to wide awake. She tried to roll over. I jumped on the hog's back and tried to keep her from getting to her feet while trying to grab the syringe with the anesthetic in it.

I was no match for the hog. She rolled over and immediately stood up. Her intestines rolled out of the open incision. I tried my best to keep her on the hay where it was somewhat clean but she wanted no part of that.

In an instant she was off the hay and running through the muck in the hog pen dragging her intestines behind her. I gave chase, syringe in hand. I finally cornered the hog and managed to give her the anesthetic injection.

After what seemed like a lifetime, she was sleeping again. I accessed the damage. The intestines were caked with mud and hog waste. Through some miracle the hog had not stepped on her intestines as she was running through the pen. With the help of the hog farmer, we put down more hay and rolled the sow on her back for the second time.

I had a water tank in my Bowie Unit and I could pump water with a fair amount of pressure through the Bowie Unit's hose. I backed my truck as close to the hog as I could and hosed down the intestinal track. I washed until I was out of water. I stuffed the intestines back into the hog's body cavity, dumped two packs of powdered antibody into the cavity and quickly closed the incision with sutures.

I gave the farmer a poor prognosis. If one microscopic drop of dirt got into the peritoneal cavity it could cause acute peritonitis (a dangerous infection in the body cavity). With all of the washing and cleaning, a huge amount of mud and manure was still mixed in with the intestines. I gave the hog a huge injection of penicillin and some follow up injections for the farmer and left the farm.

After a day or two, I called the farmer and inquired about the hog.

He said, "Doc, she's fine. She woke up hungry and hasn't missed a meal since".

I couldn't believe the news. I rode out to see her. She was still in the filthy pen, eating away. No sign of infection. I decided at that moment, try as you may, you couldn't kill a hog.

"Cry Baby"

Early in my practice, I not only treated farm animals in the field, I also treated dogs and cats. Most of my workdays were 10hrs. After coming home and relaxing, I was often called in the middle of the night for emergencies.

One night I received a call from Ms. Green. She was an elderly woman that lived alone with her Siamese cat, Cry Baby. I never asked her why she named her cat Cry Baby. I felt I already knew the answer. Siamese cats have a unique voice. It sounds very much like the cry of a human baby.

Ms. Green took excellent care of Cry Baby. He was the reason she got up each morning.

Ms. Green called about 9pm and was frantic, "Something's happened to Cry Baby".

When I asked what had happened, she said, "Cry Baby has lost a lot of weight and his eyes have turned from green to blue."

I inquired as to how long it had taken these changes to occur. She replied, "15 minutes."

Stunned, I asked again and she repeated, "15 minutes."

I knew that answer did not make sense. Ms. Green was elderly and I had started hearing about a condition called Alzheimer's Disease that affected the short-term memory of elderly people. **I** didn't want to take a chance. It could be that Cry Baby had been in a state of decline for days and she was just noticing it.

I asked her if someone could bring her to the clinic with Cry Baby. She assured me she would bring Cry Baby and would meet me at the clinic in 20 minutes.

I reached the clinic before Ms. Green so I could cut the lights on and read over Cry Baby's history. As I suspected, Cry Baby was up to date on all of his vaccinations, had been examined within the last two months and seemed to be in excellent health.

Ms. Green arrived with the very unhappy cat in a pet carrier. I removed the cat and was shocked. Before me was an old scrawny, dehydrated Siamese cat with dried skin, a dirty coat and blue eyes. Further exam showed the cat was an un-neutered male, at least 10 years old.

I rechecked Cry Baby's record which showed Cry Baby was about 4 years old, neutered and had green eyes.

I said, "Ms. Green, this isn't Cry Baby". She looked very puzzled when I explained the differences in the two cats.

She said, "Cry Baby was crying to go outside, so I let him out. 15 minutes later he was crying to get back in. When I saw how he looked, I called you."

I said, "I understand Ms. Green but this isn't Cry Baby. This is some old stray tomcat."

She said, "Then where's Cry Baby"?

I said, "Probably crying at your front door wondering why you won't let him in."

Ms. Green left with the old stray cat. I wasn't the least bit surprised when she showed up at the clinic three days later with the old tomcat. She wanted a complete exam and if the tom was healthy, she wanted all of his vaccinations and to have him neutered. I enquired about Cry Baby.

She said, "He was at the front door just as you had predicted. I've spent the last few days introducing him to the old tomcat.

I eventually told Cry Baby that I was going to keep the old tom."

She said, "Cry Baby wasn't very happy, but he'll get over it."

The Flea

Sherry and her husband Wade were two of my first clients. I met them on a horse farm when I was strictly a large animal veterinarian. They continued as clients when I switched to a mixed animal practice and again when I was strictly a small animal practitioner.

They owned two dogs, Ugh and Boo, both females. Ugh had an allergy to flea saliva and would have a scratching fit if a single flea bit her. The scratching would last for months and would keep Sherry and Wade awake at night because Ugh and Boo slept on their bed.

After exhausting my supply of approved flea control products with limited to no success in solving Ugh's problem, I placed Ugh on a monthly treatment with a product approved for use on cows only. The product is absorbed into the blood stream and is lethal to any type of insect type varmint that feeds on the medicated animals body fluids.

By giving this medication to Ugh on a monthly basis, in time Ugh and her environment would be flea and other type of varmint free. I had heard about it from product sales people at veterinary conferences. I had also spoken to many vets that were using it off the records. I knew it was safe and had used it on my four dogs for years.

 Sherry was skeptical but wanted Ugh and everyone else to be able to sleep undisturbed. I told Sherry that this was not a miracle drug and that it would take a little time before she saw the desirable effect.

Finally, determined to try this unapproved treatment she carried the product home and began administering the drug to Ugh. She called me every day with questions and wanting to know when she would see results.

Two weeks after she had administered the first treatment to Ugh she called and told she and Wade had just experienced their first night of sleep with no scratching from Ugh.

This was great news and the drug had been effective much sooner than I thought. I was elated and was happy that the daily calls from Sherry would end.

Not so. The very next day, Sherry called my office.

I asked, "Has Ugh started scratching again?"

"No" she replied, "I was just wondering what I should do if I find another flea on Ugh?"

With not a second of hesitation I answered, "If you see one, catch him and bring him to my office and I will kill him for you."

That ended the daily calls.

Sherry has since passed but Wade remained a client until I retired. Today he's one of my very best and cherished friends.

Doug

In my 35 years of practice, I met many characters. Doug was one of my favorites.

Doug was a black dairy farmer, one of only two in NC. He, his brother, their wives and their children ran the dairy. They worked very hard but it was a problem providing for the two families.

Doug had legendary strength. It was said he could lift an engine block off the ground and set it in the bed of a truck.

Doug had lost his left arm in a tractor accident. He was working behind his tractor while it was running. He reached for a tool and the "power take off" on his tractor caught the left sleeve of his shirt and continued to twist until his arm was wrenched off just below the elbow. No one else was on the farm at the time so Doug made a tourniquet with his belt and drove himself to the hospital. He lost a tremendous amount of blood. He made it to the hospital and collapsed as he entered the emergency room.

His doctor said, "A lesser man would have bled to death".

Doug used a hook to replace the arm and hand. It was the type that could open and close. He was able to pick things up and hold them but he had nowhere near the strength in the hooked hand as he did in his good hand.

I was called out to Doug's farm late one night. Doug had a cow in labor that was having trouble delivering her calf. I arrived and Doug showed me to the milking parlor. The cow was sprawled out in the parlor and couldn't get up. She had been straining for a long time. The calf was already dead and from the looks of the cow, I didn't think she would ever stand again.

My job would be to get the calf out of her without occurring too great of expense. I had a calf jack that I used on difficult births. The jack was capable of exerting a tremendous amount of pressure to remove stubborn calves or foals. Once I had the jack in position and had exerted as much pressure as I could muster, Doug's brother moved to my side. Together we exerted even greater pressure but made no progress.

Doug said, " Let me try."

He grabbed the handle of the jack and gave a mighty tug. The jack flew into pieces.

My associate had the same kind of jack on his truck. I called him and asked him to meet me about half way to the farm. We met and I took the jack from his truck and returned to Doug's dairy farm. I put the second jack in place and Doug got into position again. In a matter of minutes, Doug destroyed the second jack.

I was able to make a third jack from parts of the two broken ones. This time we didn't let Doug near. With the help of Doug's brother, I was finally able to extract the calf.

Doug was a big man but very humble. He seldom looked you in the eye and spoke with a deep southern drawl of one born to a disadvantaged life. Doug grew corn for feed for his family and his dairy cows. He leased a large strip of land from an old white woman and grew corn on the upper and lower pastures.

Corn was usually cut in the months of late May and June. One spring day a young white boy drove up to Doug's house. Doug came out to see what the young man wanted. He told Doug that he had just purchased the land Doug rented from the old white woman and he wanted Doug to harvest his corn from the pastures.

Doug told him that it was too early to harvest the corn but when it was ripe, that would be the first corn he harvested. The young man left in a huff.

The next day Doug went to the rented fields to check on his corn. The crop was in ruins. The corn stalks were crushed and lying on the ground. Tracks from four-wheel drive vehicles were all through the pastures. The corn had been deliberately run down and destroyed.

Fortunately for Doug, the crop was insured. In order for Doug to collect the insurance money, samples of the damage had to be taken by the County Extension Agent. Doug called the agent and they agreed to meet in a few hours at the damaged site.

The agent took pictures. He then took two large garbage bags for himself and gave Doug two bags. He told Doug to go down to the lower pasture and collect two bags full of the corn from the lower pasture. He collected from the upper pasture and filled out a report. Doug collected corn from the lower pasture.

A few minutes after Doug had departed, two four wheel drive pick-up trucks arrived with four young white men (one was the new land owner).

They approached the agent in a threatening manner and wanted to know why he was on this property. He tried to explain but they didn't want an explanation. They snatched the bags out of his hand and shoved him around. As he cautiously made his way back to his truck, one of thugs ripped his nametag from his shirt.

About this time, Doug was making his way out of the lower pasture. When the white boys saw Doug, they stopped their attack on the agent and stepped back. Doug continued towards the group carrying a bag of corn in each hand.

As he approached the back of his pick up truck, Doug said in his humble manner of speech, "Now boys, we don't want no trouble. We just want to take this corn and leave".

The new owner of the land, emboldened by Doug's humbleness and by the presence of his comrades, rushed towards Doug and snatched the bag of corn from Doug's hooked hand.

He threw it to the ground and hollered, "This is my land and my corn. Now get off".

Another of the boys, caught up in the moment, rushed up to Doug and tried to snatch the other bag of corn out of Doug's good hand. It was a big mistake. Doug swung the bag of corn while the boy hung on to it. The boy and the bag made a mighty arch through the air then slammed on to the back of Doug's truck. The boy and the bag of corn hit the truck's cargo space with such force that the rear of the truck shrunk down on its shock absorbers then sprang up with such force that the rear wheels lifted off of the ground.

The young boy moaned in agony. The remaining boys gathered their friend and carried him off to the hospital.

Later that evening, the sheriff came to Doug's home. The boys told the sheriff that they had come to the land and found Doug trespassing. They said they asked him what he was doing on the land and Doug attacked them with his hook.

Doug calmly told the sheriff what really happened and his story was verified by the county agent.

Those boys never bothered Doug again. He collected his insurance and used the money to buy corn for his cows.

Dr. Crow

Dr. Crow was the veterinarian that tried to fail me on the oral exam of the N.C. Boards. I had been practicing in the Gaston County area for about a year when he called.

He asked me if I had a calf jack. I told him I did.

He asked if he could borrow it. Not one to hold a grudge, I told him sure.

Then he asked me if I would bring it to his office around noon. Again, I agreed to do that.

At noon that day, I reached his office and he thanked me for the jack and said he wanted to use it to deliver a difficult foal, He said he would return the jack later in the week.

I told him I would follow him to the farm and take my jack when he had finished using it. I may need it before he could return it. He grunted and told me to follow him.

We reached the horse farm and there was a mare lying on her side staining with all she could to push out a dead foal. The owners were standing near by in tears of hopelessness as they watched their mare suffer.

Dr. Crow hooked chains to the front legs of the foal and attached the chains to the jack. He wrenched the foal out with little to no concern for the screaming mare.

Dr. Crow gave the horse a penicillin injection and prepared to leave. I asked him if I could examine the mare.

He glared at me and said, "Do what you want".

I slipped on a shoulder length plastic sleeve and did a vaginal exam on the mare. Just as I had suspected, the mare's uterus and vagina were ripped to shreds from the forceful extraction.

I walked over to Dr. Crowe and quietly informed him of my findings.

He just shrugged and said, "If she lives, she lives".

He got in his car and left. He didn't even clean the instruments he had borrowed.

As I was cleaning my instruments, the owner approached me and asked if I would help his mare. He told me he had called Dr. Crowe the night before to tell him he had a mare in labor. Dr. Crowe refused to come out that night. He told the owner that if the mare hadn't had the foal by morning to call him back and he would come out before going to his clinic.

By morning the mare and unborn foal were dead but now a second mare was in labor.

Dr. Crowe came out and examined the mare. He had the mare brought to a tree. He tied a rope around the foal's legs and the other end of the rope around the tree. He then tried to lead the horse away hoping the foal would be dragged out of the mare.

When that didn't work, he took a strap and beat the horse trying to force her to run and drag the foal out. He continued until the horse collapsed. By this time, the foal was dead.

Dr. Crow told them he was going to his clinic. He would be back at lunchtime to try again.

I was appalled. I really wanted to help the mare but told the owner I couldn't. He was Dr. Crowe's client and I couldn't in good faith interfere without Dr. Crowe's approval. I told him to ask Dr. Crowe to come back and I left.

Ten miles down the road my truck phone rang. It was the horse owner. He pleaded with me to return. He said he had called Dr. Crowe and he wouldn't come back. Dr. Crowe said he had done all he could.

I turned around and started back to the horse farm. Three miles from the ranch my phone rang again. It was my office. The ranch had called back and the mare was dead. There was no need for me to return. Dr. Crowe and I had no further contact.

I did run into the horse owner some years later. He approached me in a grocery store and spoke to me. Noticing my confusion he reminded me of the horse incident.

"Oh", I said, "Which vet are you using now?".

He said, "I still use Dr. Crowe. He's the best."

I stood there with my mouth opened. This man had lost two foals and two mares in a day's time. Dr. Crowe didn't think enough of him to make a night trip to assist a mare in labor nor did he have the compassion to try to ease the suffering of a mare who was dying from his poor practice techniques.

I walked away shaking my head and made two wishes as I left the store. (1) That I would never be as callous to my clients and patients as Dr. Crowe and (2) That I would have clients that believed in me as much as that horse client believed in Dr. Crowe.

"Levi"

Levi was one of my favorite patients. He was owned by one of my favorite clients, the Clarks. Levi was a silver, miniature Schnauzer with more human than canine characteristics. Mr. Clark was very specific about Levi's needs. Whenever they traveled, Levi went with them. If he couldn't be accommodated, the Clarks wouldn't go. The thought of leaving Levi at a boarding clinic or even at my facility with dogs was out of the question.

There came a time when the Clarks had to take a week long trip and for this trip they couldn't take Levi. They agonized over the situation until Mr. Clark thought of an acceptable solution. He commissioned Karen, my 10 year old daughter to be Levi's care person. Levi would stay at my house and Karen would be given strict instructions for Levi's care.

The day of the trip arrived. The Clarks arrived at my home with everything Levi needed. Levi had his own special water bowl and food bowl. Levi had a special bed and covers. Levi had a special diet. His snacks included Cheerios and small marshmallows. Levi was to get seven (not six or eight) Cheerios at bedtime. He was to receive four marshmallows at various hours during the day. At night, after Levi had received his Cheerios, he was to be wrapped in his blanket and laid in Karen's lap. She was to sing his favorite song, "Rudolf The Red Nosed Reindeer" to him before he was placed in his bed. Levi had lived his life more as a very pampered human rather than a dog.

Karen faithfully carried out the Clarks' meticulous instructions but there was an "X" factor in the Creed household. We owned three Jack Russell terriers. Anyone familiar with this breed knows that they are extremely hyperactive dogs.

Mine lived as a pack. They did everything together. They were friendly to other dogs so Levi was never threatened with an attack. They took all of Levi's special stuff. They preferred drinking out of Levi's bowl rather than their own.

The first night Levi spent with us, Karen had faithfully given him his seven Cheerios, wrapped him in his blanket and placed him in his bed. I received an emergency call and had to go to my clinic at three in the morning. When I reached the den where the dogs slept, all three of my Jack Russells were curled up in Levi's bed and poor Levi was sitting beside the bed, staring at them, wondering what to do.

I believed in letting my dogs work out their own problems, so I left the situation as it was and went to my clinic to see a client's sick cat. When I returned home later, Levi was comfortably curled up, sleeping soundly with my Jack Russells.

During the week of Levi's stay, he learned what it was like to be a dog. The four dogs chased squirrels, dug holes, wrestled, chewed stuff up and smelled like dogs. Levi was in seventh heaven.

When the Clarks were due to come back, I carried Levi to the clinic and cleaned him up really good. He was delighted to see his owner and jumped all over them. He licked their faces and whimpered for the love and attention that he was accustomed to in their hands.

Levi went home and I wondered if Levi would remember and miss his Jack Russell buddies.

As the years went by, the Clarks added more dogs to their canine family.

One day, Mrs. Clark came to my clinic to pick up some medication for the dogs. In our conversation, she told me of a

161

new habit her husband had developed. They now had five dogs including Levi. The Clarks lived diagonally across from a volunteer fire station.

When the station received a call, a siren would sound. Mr. Clark and the dogs would rush out on to the front porch. They were all excited but had to get in line. Each dog had its own order in the line and each had to be in place before the ritual could begin. Once everyone was in place, Mr. Clark would raise his head and howl at the siren. The dogs would join in and the howling would continue until the sirens were cut off or out of hearing range. I always wondered if Levi would retain any of the real dog traits he learned at his weeks stay with the Jack Russells. It appears he did and succeeded in teaching his owner some doggy tricks.

Billy and Carole

Artificial Insemination

Cows give milk. People take this for granted. Few people have ever thought about what it takes for cows to produce this wonderful product. A cow, just like a human must become pregnant before the right hormones are produced to cause the udder to develop. They must then have a calf before the breast can produce milk. The breast doesn't continually produce milk. Cows must be re-bred on a yearly basis to produce a continuous flow of milk.

The average dairy farm's cows are divided into three categories: the milking herd (cows actively producing milk and milked twice per day), dry cows (cows getting ready to give birth are given a rest period from active milking for six weeks or more before their calving date), and heifers (a female cow until she has her first calf). The ideal ratio is 2:1:1. When calves are born, the females are raised to replace the cows whose milk production has dropped to an undesirable level for one reason or another.

Heifers become fertile at about nine to twelve months of age. They haven't reached their full development at this age so dairymen wait until they are eighteen months old to breed them. Bull calves are neutered, sold and raised for beef.

When I started my practice, just about all of the dairies were using artificial insemination to breed their cows. Most dairy farms did not own a bull. They bought frozen semen from companies that breed and collect semen from the top bulls from all over the world. Each semen sample is stored in a small plastic container referred to as a straw. The commercial companies draw diluted semen into these straws and seal each end with a synthetic plug.

163

The straw containers are the length and width of a toothpick. They are stored in dry ice containers from the commercial companies and brought to the dairy farms. The dairymen pick the semen they want to use in their herd and the semen is transferred to their personal dry ice containers until the dairyman is ready to breed a cow.

To breed a cow through artificial insemination, the semen must be placed into the cow's uterus by the use of an inseminating rod. The inseminating rod consists of a metal barrel and plunger. It is 18 inches long and has a diameter about half the diameter of a pencil.

When a cow is in heat, the dairyman thaws the appropriate straw of semen and clips off one of the plugged ends. The plunger of the rod is removed and the straw is dropped into the barrel (clipped off end first). The barrel is tapered so that the straw will not pass through the far end of the barrel. The plunger is then re-inserted into the barrel until it reaches the plugged end of the straw.

A protective plastic sleeve is then placed over the inseminating rod (this protects the cows sensitive inner parts from scratches and contamination from other cows). The dairyman then puts a shoulder length plastic sleeve over his left arm and places the sleeved rod in his mouth. The cow to be bred has been placed in a holding chute. The dairyman reaches into the rectum of the cow with his sleeved left hand and arm and searches for the cow's cervix (the size and texture of half a corn cob). He then removes the rod from his mouth and gently works the rod through the cow's vaginal area to the opening of the cervix. The rod must then be worked completely through the cervix (this can sometimes be difficult). Once the rod is completely through the cervix, the semen can be injected into the uterus. The cow has now been bred by artificial insemination. The success rate is less than 30%.

Billy and Carole are dairy farmers. They milk about 200 Holstein cows. Billy is the quiet one of the two. Carole has all of the answers and dominates Billy. They have two sons that help with the milking, farming and the hundreds of chores it takes to run a successful dairy. Of the 200 cow herd there are usually 50 heifers waiting to reach the age of breeding.

Billy had just completed a course in artificial insemination. He had ordered and received his storage tank and it had been charged with dry ice. He had recently purchased several straws of quality semen and an inseminating rod. A couple of his cows were in heat and he asked me to come to his dairy while he attempted his first try at inseminating a cow.

The cow was in the chute. Billy's wife Carole and their two kids were there to witness this great new step in producing better cows. Billy carefully extracted the selected straw of semen from his tank and dropped it in a cup of water to thaw. He removed the plunger from his inseminating rod, took the straw from the water with forceps designed to hold the straw and wiped the straw dry.

He clipped off one end of the straw and expertly placed it in the barrel of the inseminating rod with the clipped end down just as he had been instructed. He replaced the plunger and slipped the protective plastic sleeve over the inseminating rod. He placed the rod in his mouth as he put a shoulder length plastic glove on his left hand and arm. He approached the cow and gently inserted his arm into the cow's rectum.

He felt around a little and then smiled as he said; "I've found the cervix". He next removed the rod from his mouth with his right hand and gently eased the rod into the cow's vagina and up to the mouth of the cervix. Now he was trying to work the rod completely through the cervix and he was beginning to struggle. After a very long attempt he removed the rod from the cow's vagina and placed it back in his mouth.

Every one but Billy realized what he had just done. We were collectively holding our breaths. Billy continued this procedure completely unaware of what he had just done.

After an uncomfortable pause, Carole said, "Billy, you're going to have to brush your teeth before you give me any sugar tonight."

I fell to the ground with laughter as did his boys. It took Billy a minute to realize what we were laughing about. Undaunted, he continued with his task and successfully completed his first attempt at inseminating a cow.

The "B"

The dairy business is quite complicated. You have to be part herdsman, part veterinarian, part machinist, part mechanic, part farmer, part accountant and completely out of your mind. You milk cows twice per day, seven days per week. Christmas is just another milk day but you get turkey for dinner. Dairymen are up around 4 am and go to bed around 9pm. They are usually exhausted from a day"s work that most of us would cringe at the thought of doing. Billy was an excellent dairyman. The amazing part of this is Billy couldn't read or write. Very few people knew this outside of his family.

One day when I was on the farm to examine some cows, Carole quietly came up to me and said; "Don't say anything to Billy but he's going back to school to learn how to read. He wants the boys to be proud of him".

I smiled and said, "That's great Carole but I'd bet the boys are already proud of him."

It was my job to examine the cows and tell them which ones were pregnant, which were ready to turn dry and which were ready to breed. I kept a large waxed pencil on me and marked a "B" if they were to be bred and "D" if it was time to turn them dry.

When the first cow came through, I told them this cow could be bred that day. I pulled out my pen to mark a big "B" on the cow when Billy said, "Let me do that".

He walked up to me, took the waxed pencil and printed a large "D" on the cow's side.

Carole hollered out, "That's a "D", you dummy".

Billy slowly handed me the waxed pencil and I never heard any more about his learning to read or write again.

Da Bull

Billy and Carole's neighbor, John, raises Angus beef cows. The Angus breed is a short stocky solid black animal that is bred for the main purpose of producing meat. It is quite different from the Holstein breed that is much taller, develops a large udder and is primary a milk producer.

John is a weekend farmer and lives in the city. His farm bordered Billy and Carole's farm. The two farms are separated by a few strands of barbwire fence. John owns a bull.

When Billy and Carole's heifers come in heat, it drives John's bull crazy. One day the bull broke through the fence and bred some of the Holstein heifers. This is a real bad situation. The female calves from this breeding would not be suitable to replace pure bred Holstein cows. So a year is lost on this wasted breeding.

Carole and her sons caught the bull, carried it back to John's farm, tied it so it couldn't escape, patched the fence and left John a note telling him what happened. They would appreciate him doing something to assure this wouldn't happen again.

A week later, the bull was back. This time Carole kept the bull on her farm. She left a note that John could pick up his bull after he patched the fence and paid them $300.00 for their trouble.

John did as the letter suggested and picked up his bull with an embarrassed apology.

Two weeks later the bull was back again. Carole was furious. She tied the bull in her pasture and left a threatening letter. If John ever wanted to see his bull again, he had better fix the fence so the bull couldn't get through or move the bull away from their pasture. He had until three o'clock that afternoon to reply or she was going to take his bull to market and sell it for beef.

At three o'clock, Carole had her sons load the bull into a trailer and off to market she went. She sold the bull for $700.00 and brought the check home.

Around ten that night John showed up at Billy and Carole's door demanding his bull. Carole offered him the check from the stockyard. John refused to take the check and stormed off.

Around mid-night the county sheriff showed up at Carole's door. John had told the sheriff that he had come to his farm and found his bull missing. When he asked around the area about his bull, someone had seen Carole hauling a bull that could have been his in a trailer. When he went to her home to inquire on this matter, Carole tried to give him a check made out to her from the stockyard.

He made it sound as if Carole had stolen his bull, sold it, and offered him the money only after she had been caught.

Carole was a hot head and started screaming at the sheriff. The sheriff arrested her and hauled her off to jail as Billy watched in silence.

Seven o'clock the next morning, Billy called me at home and told me what had happened. Billy couldn't read or write and was intimidated by government so he wanted me to go down to the jail and bail Carole out. I asked, "Why didn't you call me last night?"

He said, "I didn't want to wake you up."

I said, "You let your wife stay in jail all night because you didn't want to wake me?"

169

I said, "I'll go get her but she's going to make mincemeat out of you when I bring her home."

I dressed, went to the jailhouse, paid Carole's bail. I carried her to breakfast so she would calm down before I carried her home.

To my surprise, she was very calm. She didn't seem upset at Billy at all.

While we were eating I asked, "Carole, you don't seem angry that you had to spend a night in jail?"

She smiled and said, "George, Billy snores something awful. That's the best nights sleep I've had in many a year. I might do something else so I can go back."

Carole had to find out who bought John's bull and buy it back. It probably cost her a lot more than she had been paid.

About a month later I was on the farm to treat some cows and asked if the bull ever came back.

She looked at me with a knowing smile and said; "Yea, once. But then he just disappeared". Nothing more was ever said but Billy, Carole and their two sons ate a lot of steak over the next few weeks.

James

James Shoven was my first associate veterinarian. He was a few years younger than me and a Jewish guy from an affluent family in New York He had attended veterinary school in Italy. While there, he met and married Mariah, an Italian Catholic woman and the love of his life.

James had come to my house to meet me and ask if I would consider helping him. In order to receive a license to practice veterinary medicine in the US, James was required to complete a year's internship program. Six months with a veterinarian practicing small animal medicine (pet practice) and six months with a veterinarian practicing large animal medicine (farm animals) would be required.

Small animal vets were a dime a dozen but large animal vets were rare. He had received a residency offer with one of the local small animal veterinarians. He had heard from the area veterinarians that I was the only one in the area practicing large animal medicine.

James and his wife were sitting in my den talking with my wife when I returned home from a farm call.

When James saw me for the first time, he leaned over to his wife and whispered to her in Italian, "My God! He's whiter than me".

Actually, James and I are the same complexion. He is taller, has very curly hair, a mustache and beard. He explained his situation to me. I really didn't need any help. The way I worked, he would actually slow me down. My work in reproduction was very specialized. He would have to travel with me and I would have to teach him what I do.

I told him I could let him ride with me one day/ week if that would help. He contacted the NC Veterinary Board and was told one week with me was equivalent to a full week with any other vet. James finished his internship, passed his boards and was licensed. I hired him as an associate veterinarian and that was the start of a life long friendship.

I had more work than a single vet could handle in large animals but not enough for two. I decided to expand my business to include dogs and cats. James' main responsibility was to start a small animal branch to our large animal business.

We leased a small building at a crossroad on the western outskirt of Dallas, NC We hired two ladies to assist us in surgery, treating, restraining animals, taking calls, keeping records and making appointments.

James trained these ladies and was basically in charge of the small animal business. I spent the mornings working on herd reproduction with the dairies. We alternated work in the small animal practice in the evenings. One week I would be in the clinic and James would take large animal calls and after hour emergency calls. The next week we switched. We were busy and business was good.

One day a woman was in the clinic and I was on duty. When I walked into the examination room, she looked closely at me and asked, "Which one are you? You're both dark."

Without hesitation I answered, "No, he's dark. I'm light". She looked at me puzzled. I said; "Think about it. It'll come to you."

I was finished with my large animal calls for the day and called into the clinic to see if there was anything else I needed to do before I came in. As I was driving through Boger City, I passed what is usually an empty field. Today it contained a group of men dressed in hooded sheets and burning a cloth covered cross.

172

I stopped talking in mid sentence. James asked, "Is anything wrong?"

I said, "You won't believe what I'm looking at."

When I described the scene, he jokingly asked, "Is anyone on it?"

I said, "Don't be so dismissive. When they get rid of all of my people, they're coming for yours."

The only other time I was made aware of the Ku Klux Klan presence in this area was when I was driving to a dairy in Crouse, NC .I was crossing a bridge. Pinned to the bridge was a poorly written sign reading, "Klan meeting this Saturday night. No niggers allowed". It gave the time and place. I wanted that sign but didn't want anyone to see me take it. Every time I stopped my truck, a car or truck approached and I would jump back in the truck and pull off. I circled around and tried again. After the third try, I retrieved it. I carried it home and eventually gave it to my father-in-law as a souvenir.

My front yard is full of large oak trees. I love the shade but pay dearly for the trees every fall when the leaves cover my lawn like a thick brown blanket. My yearly tradition is to rake the leaves into a huge pile in the middle of the front lawn. Then I would turn my three children loose and they would dive into the leaf pile along with the dogs. After they tired of the leaves, I gathered the leaves and spread them in a natural area in the back yard.

One fall after hours of raking, I decided to burn them instead of moving them. Again, I gathered them into a huge pile in the front yard. I lit the pile and watched it burn. When the fire finally burned out, it left a large circular charred area in the middle of my front yard. My wife made me promise to never do that again. The charred area remained through the winter and into early spring.

One April morning one of my dairy clients stopped by the house to pick up some medication for his cows. He noticed the charred circular area in the front yard and inquired about it.

Being in a jovial mood, I answered, "The Klan came by last week and burnt a cross in the yard".

His face filled with surprise and anger. He said, "Dr. Creed, I think that's terrible. We think you and your family are fine people. I would be proud to live next door to you".

Now I was embarrassed. This normally quiet man that I had known for five years seldom said more than two words when I was on his dairy farm. I had never seen him show any emotion in the past and now he was truly upset.

I apologized and told him I was just joking. The neighbors were fine and the Klan had never bothered us. He showed a small smile, ducked his head and walked away. I never joked with him again.

Rosemary

In my 35 years of practice, I ran into many interesting cases, One of my most interesting was an emu named Rosemary. An emu is a large bird native to Australia. It looks very much like an ostrich. Emus weigh approximately 120 lbs. and stand six feet tall. They have undeveloped wings so they can't fly. They have very powerful legs and can outrun most predators. Their bodies are covered with a substance that resembles hair rather than feathers.

One Saturday morning, I received a call from Pharr Aviary in McAdenville (a small town about 15 miles fro my clinic). It was the property of the millionaire owner of Pharr Yarn Textile Mill. Mr. Pharr loved birds and had amassed an amazing collection of native and exotic birds. He liked to go out to his aviary and have one of his servants bring him lunch while he was with his birds. He opened the aviary to the public one-day a week. For the rest of the week, only he and the animal keepers were allowed on the premises.

I was called shortly after the aviary had purchased Rosemary, a female emu. Rosemary was lying around, not eating and seemed depressed. I informed the caller that I didn't know anything about emus but I would come and examine her anyway.

When I reached the aviary, I was escorted to large fenced area. The enclosure was 2 ½ acres. There were two emu in the enclosure; Ralph (a male that had lived several years on the premises) and Rosemary (their latest purchase). The hope was that Ralph and Rosemary would breed and supply the aviary with little emus.

When I approached Rosemary, she was sitting on her haunches. Even sitting, she was an impressive sight. I was intimidated by the size of this bird. I was very alarmed at the size of its beak. Put your hands together as if you were going to pray. Look at your hands and that will give you the approximate size of her beak.

I asked the keeper, "How does she fight?"

He looked puzzled so I said, "How does she defend herself? Does she peck, spit or bite?"

He said, "Doc, she kicks like a mule. If you can grab her while she's sitting and keep her from getting to her feet, I think you can examine her."

I came closer to Rosemary and she was now at full alert. I could tell she was getting anxious as I approached. I began circling her and she kept her eyes on me. My plan was to jump on her back and grab her neck just below her head to keep her from pecking or biting me.

The problem was Rosemary could turn her head around 180 degrees. She would then snap it around so quickly that no matter how I circled, she was always looking directly at me and I was looking at that tremendous beak. I eventually gathered the courage to attack. I charged the bird, leaped on her back and grabbed the neck as planned. That's as far as I had planned. Now what can I do? I was afraid to let go of Rosemary's neck. How could I examine her?

Rosemary solved that problem. She stood up as if my weight was as insignificant as a fly. She shook herself much as a wet dog shakes when it has been submerged in water. I was thrown to the ground. I pulled myself up from the dirt and was standing there trying to decide my next course of action. Suddenly, Rosemary leaped into the air and placed a powerful side-kick directly into my abdomen. Bruce Lee, Steven Stegal, Chuck Norris and Jean Claude Van Damme would have given Rosemary a standing ovation for such a well-placed kick.

The air rushed out of me. I was flat on my back and more embarrassed than hurt. The keeper tried his best to look concerned but could not prevent a soft giggle from escaping his lips.

Rosemary was off and running at full gallop. I went back to my truck and retrieved my lasso. Rosemary had crossed the line. Now this was a personal matter and I was determined to complete the exam of this "martial arts" avian. The keeper and I chased Rosemary through the compound for over an hour trying to corner her in a position so I could throw the lasso.

"This bird can't be sick if it can run like this", I thought. Finally Rosemary tired and I had my chance. Rosemary had run into a corner of the compound just as the keeper and I arrived. She paused long enough for me to throw my lasso.

Just as the loop of the lasso passed over Rosemary's head, she took off again (before I snatched the lasso hoping the loop would close around Rosemary's neck). She was too fast. By the time I snatched my end of the rope, the loop had cleared her neck, her body and was now around her legs. As I pulled tight, the loop closed around Rosemary's ankles and snatched her off of her feet.

Rosemary went down with a huge thud that knocked the wind out of her. I was on her in a flash, wrapping the rope around her legs so she was unable to rise. The keeper came to my assistance and sat on her to keep her from regaining her up-right position.

Finally, I could take my time and examine Rosemary. It didn't take long to find the cause of her symptoms. Rosemary had bruises all over her body I examined the cloaca (birds urinate and defecate through one opening called the cloaca). I found something Ralph the emu must have noticed when Rosemary first arrived. Rosemary was a male.

Ralph was the larger of the two. The aviary was his domain and he would fight another male to establish dominance. He had caused the bruises on Rosemary and that is why she/he laid around in submission. Ralph would not allow the new bird to eat or walk around his domain without attacking. Rosemary was sent back to his original farm and a new female was sent to Pharr's aviary.

I was not called back so I assume all went well. I hope they remembered to change Rosemary's name.

Precious

I was attending church in Lincoln Co. when I met Edith, the matriach of our small 40-member church. She had never married nor had children. She lived on her family property which boasted 50 acres of mostly wooded land. Edith always had a large garden. Even at her advanced age, she did the planting, weeding and harvesting.

One evening while tending the garden, she found a small female kitten barely big enough to cover her hand. The right front leg dangled uselessly at its side. She carried it to her car, rushed to my clinic and waited patiently for me to exam the kitten.

The kitten's front leg had probably been damaged while the kitten was still in the womb. The leg was nothing but bones covered by skin. All of the muscles and vessels were missing. My guess is the umbilical chord had wrapped around the leg and strangulated the vessels while the kitten was still in the womb.

When I explained this to Edith, I suggested that we should amputate the useless limb.

Edith was horrified and said, "No George. You have to save her leg".

This was not going to happen. The leg would be in the way as the kitten tried to run and play. I finally convinced her of this and tried to lighten the situation by saying, "We can amputate the leg and name her Tri-pod".

Edith looked me straight in the eyes and said with a firm voice, "Her name is Precious".

Precious quickly became the child Edith never had. She loved Precious and took excellent care of her. Precious did not care for visitors and would hide when Edith had company and stay hidden until the company was gone.

As time passed, Edith was diagnosed with an advanced stage of breast cancer. As she went through the treatments that were available, the church rallied around her. Church members made sure she got to her doctor appointments. She received nourishing foods and had someone to cook and clean for her at all times.

Precious learned to tolerate other people in her home as Edith's condition deteriorated. A year into her illness, a nephew from the West Coast showed up at her door. He moved into her house and quickly eliminated the church members' care. He convinced Edith to give him power of attorney for her health and finances. Once he had this control, he put Edith in an assisted living facility and then he moved back to the West Coast.

As with most of our church members, I visited Edith on a regular basis. She knew she was not long for this world. On every one of my visits, Edith would say to me, "Now George, when I'm gone, I want you to promise me that you will take care of Precious".

I would try to counter with some statement like, "Oh Edith, you'll probably out live me".

She would take my hands, pull me close, stare me in the eyes and say with as much force as she could muster, "Say you will do it. I want to hear you say you will take care of Precious."

I would give in and say with tears in my eyes and trembling lips, "Yes Edith. I will take care of Precious."

Edith would let go of my hands; close her eyes and say, "Good! Now go home and let an old lady rest."

We didn't see the nephew again until the day of Edith's funeral. He showed up. As was his nature, he put himself in charge of the service even though he had made none of the arrangements.

When the service was over, I approached him and told him I was going to take Precious to live with me.

He said, "Oh no! I'm taking her back West to give to my daughter. She already has another name for her."

Not wanting to make a scene at the moment, I just stepped away. I approached Wynona, Edith's neighbor and good friend. Wynona had the keys to Edith's house and had taken care of Precious while Edith was in the assisted living facility. I asked Wynona if I could borrow Edith's keys. She asked me why and I told her about my promise to Edith and the conversation I had just had with the nephew.

She asked, "What are you going to do?"

I said, "I'm going to get Precious."

She said, "I'll go with you."

I said, "No! What I'm about to do is against the law and I don't want to get you in trouble."

She said, "I've been taking care of her. She'll come to me but hide from you."

I relented and together we stole Precious. As I put her in a carrying case to transport her home, Wynona asked me, "What are you going to say when the nephew asks you about the cat?"

I answered, "WHAT CAT?"

Precious is alive and well. She lives a life of luxury and she will probably outlive me.

Precious in her surgery gown

Old John

Mr. McCoy was a veterinarian's nightmare. He was a grumpy old man that was never satisfied with any thing. Each time I drove to his farm, he met me at his driveway with a look of impatience and disgust on his face. He complained about my prices. He complained about the weather. He complained about life in general. He was the most negative person I'd ever met. I always left his farm feeling down and depressed.

Mr. McCoy lived alone. Gossip in the area said Mr. McCoy's wife and children left him a long time ago. I'd always wondered if this created Mr. McCoy's nasty disposition or if his disposition attribute to their leaving.

Mr. McCoy had a few cows, some chickens, pigs, ducks and an old mule named John. Mr. McCoy treated his animals well but never owned a companion animal like a dog or a cat.

One Monday morning, I received a call from Mr. McCoy, "Please come quick". He said, "John is very sick".

Did Mr. McCoy actually say "please"? I had never heard him use that word. As I drove to his farm, I tried to prepare myself for the despair that always came with a McCoy farm visit. When I arrived, Mr. McCoy was in his driveway at his usual position, but something was very different. Mr. McCoy had a nervous, anxious look on his face. There was deep concern in his voice and I swear there was a tear in his eye.

As he led me to his barn to see John, he explained, "Friday evening, a neighbor asked me if he could use John to pull up a tree stump. I thought the exercise might be good for John. He has lived a life of luxury and hasn't done a lick of work in years. My neighbor picked John up Friday morning and didn't return him till late Saturday evening. On Sunday John wouldn't eat and wouldn't leave his stall. This morning he's lying down and won't get up. Doc, there's blood coming out when he pees".

Mr. McCoy continued, "Doc, I've owned Old John for more than 20 years and he was already old when I bought him. I don't have any family. John is the only thing I love. Doc, you've got to fix him".

My heart went out to Mr. McCoy, but I knew before I even examined John what I was going to find. John had azoturia. It is commonly called "Monday Morning Sickness". I saw this condition a lot when I was in school in Alabama. Many of the farmers in rural Alabama worked regular jobs during the week-days and on their farms on week-ends. Lots of them over worked these animals on the week-ends and by Monday morning, they were down and couldn't get up. The condition is similar to muscle cramps but much worse. The muscles break down releasing large amounts of lactic acid causing severe pain. The acid crystalizes in the kidneys causing blood in the urine.

The outcome is almost always fatal. I treated John the best I could. I gave him large volumes of fluids to dilute the acid in hope of allowing the kidneys to handle a diluted toxin. I gave Mr. McCoy follow up medicine to keep John out of pain and gave him a poor prognosis.

I told Mr. McCoy, "Keep John sitting up and make sure he gets plenty of water." Then I said, Mr. McCoy, this is a very bad condition. If John is unable to rise in three days, he probably never will. If that happens, call me and I will come back and put John down."

Mr. McCoy's head was down. He didn't look up when he said," I understand Doc. But if that time comes, I'll handle it myself." He paid me and I left the farm depressed as usual. However this time it was for a different reason.

Three or four months went by before I heard from Mr. McCoy again. On the phone he was his usual unpleasant self. He wanted me to examine a cow that wasn't doing well.

When I arrived, he was at his usual station in the driveway and his disposition was as sour as ever.

Before he told me about his cow, I asked, "What ever happened to John?"

His attitude immediately softened. He said, " Doc, I did just as you told me. I kept John propped up and tried to feed him and give him water. But he wouldn't eat unless I put the grain in his mouth. He wouldn't drink unless it was from my hands. I worked with him for two days with no sign of improvement."

He continued, "On the third day when I went to the barn, he was still down. I'll be honest with you Doc. I held his head and cried for a long time. I finally got up, told him goodbye and went to the house to get my rifle. When I came back out on the porch, there was Old John standing by the steps. John even walked around to show me he was all right. He's been eating and drinking ever since. Doc, he won't even lie down to go to sleep. He just leans against the shed. Doc, ya reckon Old John understood what I was about to do?"

I answered, " Yea, I reckon."

From that time on, whenever Mr. McCoy was unpleasant, all I had to do to change his disposition was to ask, "How's Old John?"

"Mama Didn't Raise No Fool"

11pm **one** night, I received a call from Tom Long. He told me he had been out of town for a few days and his upon return, found one of his horses missing. He searched his farm and found the horse tied to a tree nearly starved to death.

I got directions to his Mt. Holly farm, dressed and headed out. Mr. Long was beside the road with another man. He flagged me down with his flashlight.

He said, "She's out in the woods, Doc".

We crossed the street, went through a pasture and into the woods. When we reached the horse, I had to step back. Immediately alarms went off in my head. I was in a dangerous situation. When he said the horse was tied to a tree, I expected that the horse had a halter or a rope around its neck with the other end around the tree.

What I saw was an extremely emaciated red roan (spattered reddish color) mare, lying on her side She had her front feet tied together, back feet tied together and the front feet and the back feet tied together around the trunk of a tree.

I assessed my situation. Here I was in the middle of the woods with two white men I didn't know. I knew they had lied to get me out here. I always carried a pistol when I went out at night and tonight was no exception. I was torn for a moment as to whether or not to pull my pistol and escape the situation or to wait and see how the situation played out.

Why was I alarmed? Put yourself in Mr. Long's position. If you found your horse tied in the woods in this manner, what would be your first response?

You would cut her loose. You certainly wouldn't leave her tied like that while you called a vet and then waited for the vet to arrive.

Next, if someone had tied a horse up like that, even in a weakened condition, she would try to get up. There were no rope burns on her legs. The ground was undisturbed and there were no marks of any kind on the horse to indicate a struggle.

I cut the horse loose and examined her. My concern for myself shifted to concern about this poor animal. She was severely dehydrated and her responses to my poking and prodding were minimal at best, She was dying. My exam revealed that she was also pregnant. I couldn't elicit movement from the foal so there was a good chance that it was already dead inside of her.

I stood up and told Mr. Long that this was bad. The horse was probably beyond saving and she had suffered enough. The kindest thing to do was to "put her down."

He understood but answered, "Try anyway. If anyone asks you, you've done the best you can do and I've done everything I can do."

I worked on that horse for the next two hours. I gave her IV fluids , vitamins and proteins. While working on the mare, a young yearling foal approached us. It was also dehydrated and very thin. It stayed near watching us work on the mare. I realized that this was the mare's foal from last year and the mare was probably still nursing this yearling.

This was really bad. This poor mare was starving. The foal inside of her and the yearling foal were drawing away any nutrient reserves she might have had for her own survival.

When I had done all I could do, I told Mr. Long that if she lived through the night, give me a call and I'll come back and give her more fluids. I gave him a bill, he paid me and I left his farm.

Three days later, I received a call at 6 am from Gaston County Animal Control. They had received three calls from people on their way to work saying they had observed a horse lying beside the road in very bad shape. The Animal Control officer didn't know the owner of the horse but gave me directions to the site.

I knew the site. It was Mr. Long's farm. When I reached the site, several cars were parked along the road. I could see the Animal Control truck and an officer on the roadside near a tarp covering a large object. Mr. Long was there and rushed to my truck as I exited it.

He said, "Doc, she improved for awhile but I guess it was too much for her and she died."

I told him I was sorry and tried to step around him to take a look at the horse.

Mr. Long blocked my way and said, "She's dead Doc, You might as well leave."

I tried again to step around him and again he blocked my way. I knew that for some reason, he didn't want me to see the animal under the tarp.

Remembering what he had tried to pull on me the first night I met him, I was determined to see what was under the tarp.

I said, "I guess you're right." I turned to get into my truck and he relaxed. I didn't get in the truck, I took a wide step as I turned 360 degrees and was past him and on my way to the tarp covered animal.

188

He was hot on my heels hollering for me to stop. The officer heard the commotion and immediately responded. The officer was on full alert and rapidly got between Mr. Long and me. He had his hand on his pistol but kept it holstered.

I knew I was safe so I reached the tarp and pulled it away. There laid a sorrel gelding (neutered male horse). It was dead but certainly not the horse I had examined three days earlier.

When I stated that fact, Mr. Long was in total denial. He said, "Doc, you're wrong. This is the same horse. You see so many that you're confused."

I turned from the horse and crossed the street. I was heading across the pasture and into the woods where the starving mare had been.

Mr. Long was hot on my trail screaming, "This is private property. You are trespassing. You have no right."

The Animal Control officer kept between us and let me continue into the woods. There in the clearing was the dead mare. The young yearling was also dead.

The Animal Control officer and I walked throughout the woods finding lots of dead horses, cows and pigs. All appeared as if they had starved to death. We found a variety of 15 dead animals and 4 animals barely alive.

I turned to the officer and said, "Arrest him!" The officer said he didn't have the authority to arrest him but he gave him a citation and called to have the few living animals removed from the farm. He also took pictures to document the event.

Months later, I was called to court for a hearing on Mr. Long's case. I had to wait because there was another case being handled when I arrived for court. Judge Ramseur was presiding. He had just sentenced a man to 60 days in jail.

The man wailed, "No Judge! I'm sorry. I just can't do 60 days."

Judge Ramseur smiled, leaned way over his bench and said in a measured tone, "Well son, you just do the best you can."

The whole court erupted in laughter. I liked this Judge.

It was now time for Mr. Long's case. I was sworn in and took the stand. I told the judge what I had observed and what I felt caused the death of so many animals. It was plain and simple. This was an extreme example of criminal neglect.

Mr. Long stared at me through out my entire testimony. If looks could kill, I would certainly have been dead. When he took the stand in his defense, he told the judge the he was a bachelor. There were times that he would take short vacations from his farm but he always left someone to take care of the animals. He always left money for that person to buy food. He had done the same thing on this occasion.

The man left in charge didn't take care of the animals and that wasn't his fault. The man he had hired was named Bob.

Unknown to Mr. Long, the prosecuting attorney knew about Bob and produced him as the next witness. Bob was called to the stand and sworn in. He said he frequently took care of Mr. Long's animals when Mr. Long would take trips. On this occasion, Mr. Long said he would be gone for a week or two. He gave Bob enough money for about a weeks worth of food and told him that if the animals ran out of food, they could graze until he returned.

Mr. Long was away for four months. It was winter and the grass in the pastures had died. When the money ran out, Bob stopped going to the farm assuming Mr. Long would return shortly and care for his own animals. Mr. Long never left a

190

forwarding address and he really had no idea where he had gone (cell phones were not around at this time).

It was a no brainer for the judge. He found Mr. Long guilty of gross neglect, fined him $500.00 and ruled that he couldn't own an animal for six months. I was disappointed at the light sentence but knew the jails were full of humans with crimes against humans. Animals were considered property. Jail time was seldom issued in these cases.

Mr. Long was furious. When the trial was over, he rushed toward me, pointing his finger at me and hollering, "You're a dead man Creed. You're a dead man."

The judge had not left the courtroom and heard the remarks. He turned and took his place back on the bench. He hammered his gavel and the room grew quiet. He told everyone to sit down.

He starred at Mr. Long for a long time and said with his voice trembling with anger, "You've got to be the biggest fool I've ever met. You threaten a man in my courtroom in my presence. You better pray nothing ever happens to Dr. Creed. If he walks out in the middle of the street with a car bearing down on him, you'd better push him out of the way and take the hit yourself. This whole court heard you threaten him so if he ever has an accident, I'm going to assume you caused it and I'll put you away forever. For that matter, let's start today. I sentence you to one week in jail for the audacity of communicating a threat in my courtroom."

Yes I can truthfully say, "My mama didn't raise no fools". To bad Mr. Long can't say the same about his mama.

The Stolen Watch

I got to work at my usual time 7:15 am. The clinic opens at 7:30 am and I liked to get there early enough to evaluate any animals that had stayed overnight. As I arrived through the back door there was a woman banging frantically on the glass front door. Thinking this was an emergency; I rushed to open the front door.

Mrs. Walker was standing there out of breath. She had her Cocker Spaniel, Daisy, with her. She said, "Daisy needs a bath."

I stood there flabbergasted, but I had already let her in. I lifted Daisy and carried her to the back of the clinic and placed her in a cage. I told one of the technicians to check her in.

When I returned to the reception area, Mrs. Walker asked when her dog would be ready. I told her we would wash Daisy in a few minutes but she needed to stay under the drier for an hour or so. I told her she could get Daisy any time after noon.

She looked at her wrist and exclaimed, "Oh no! My watch is missing!"

I looked around the reception area and didn't see it. I checked my pockets because I had carried Daisy back and it might have come off when I took the dog. I went back and checked Daisy but found no watch. I walked with Ms. Walker back to her car and we searched all around the car and the clinic grounds but no watch. I suggested that she look for it at home.

As she left she told me, "The watch is a Timex. It didn't cost much but had sentimental value."

An hour passed and Mrs. Walker called. She said," I'll be there to get Daisy at noon and I want my watch."

I said, "Mrs. Walker, we looked for your watch and it isn't here."

She answered, ' I'm telling you when I come to get my dog, you'd better have my watch."

I grew angry and told her to come get her dog right then.

She drove up a half an hour later. Her son was with her. He stood six feet three and weighed about 230lbs.

I went to the back of the clinic and took Daisy out of her cage. She was soaking wet. I carried her back to the reception area and as Mrs. Walker and her hulking son came through the door, I stuck the wet dog in the son's arms and told them to leave.

Mrs. Walker said, "Don't think this is over".

Her son asked, "Why did you steal my mother's watch".

I just stared him and said, "Get out".

They left but I was pacing the floor with anger. As the day went on and I attended other clients, I forgot the matter.

At two o'clock pm a deputy from the sheriff's office entered the clinic and asked to see me in private.

I led him to my office and he informed me that Mrs. Walker had taken out a complaint against me, accusing me of stealing her watch. I was dumbfounded but explained the details of the incident to him. I showed him the nice Seiko watch I was wearing.

He smiled and said, "She acted sort of strange like she was on medication or something else." He apologized for any inconvenience and told me the matter was over as far as he was concerned.

I didn't hear from Mrs. Walker for six years. She walked into the clinic one day and asked to speak with me in private. I led her to my office and she asked if I remembered her. I did.

She said, "I found my watch later that evening on the top of my commode and I'm sorry that I accused you of stealing it."

I stood there without saying a word. I knew something else was coming. Why was she here after six years and what did she want?

She then asked, "Can I bring Daisy back to your clinic. The veterinarian I use charges too much."

I told her, "I accept your apology but I will not allow you to be a client again."

She looked shocked and said, 'I told God about this and He has forgiven me. I don't understand why you won't."

I answered, "Mrs. Walker, I'm a Christian. I talk to God on a daily basis, but He has never once mentioned your name to me. The day He does, you can come back."

Needless to say, I never saw Mrs. Walker, her hulking son or Daisy again.

My Strangest Cases

The Storm

I had a client that owned a beautiful Pit Bull dog named "Lulu". Lulu was a sweet dog. She never met a stranger and loved everyone she met. Her predominant color was white, but she had broad splotches of deep brown and black markings.

Joe, her owner made sure she got the best of care. When she was two years old, Joe decided to breed her. He chose a male that complemented her size and attitude.

I examined Lulu when she was "in heat"(a three week period that occurs twice per year when female dogs are fertile and receptive to males). I told Joe the optimum time to breed his dog and she conceived. Joe was happy and anxiously awaited Lulu's delivery date.

Then tragedy struck. In the late 80's, Hurricane Hugo hit our area with a force greater than any storm in my lifetime. Power was out for days. The area was a disaster zone. Fences were down, cows were loose, horses were running loose, and Lulu was missing.

Joe was devastated not knowing what had happened. Lulu's whelping date was at hand and she was missing. Joe didn't know if someone had found her or if she had been killed or was just confused and lost because of the devastated surroundings. Maybe she just didn't recognize where she was.

He looked for her constantly. He placed ads in the newspaper and offered a large reward for her return. Three weeks had passed since the storm.

Miraculously, Lulu returned home. She was dirty, very thin and obviously not pregnant. Joe brought her to my office. He told me she wouldn't eat.

Initially I thought she had delivered her pups during the storm in some hidden place and stayed with them until they died. A mother dog would not leave her pups for long if they were alive. That would explain her condition and why she was away so long.

As I examined her, she seemed painful in her abdominal area. I radiographed her abdomen and saw multiple pups still inside of her. I told Joe but couldn't explain why she looked so thin. I also knew Lulu was weeks pass her due date.

I had Lulu prepped for surgery and Joe waited in the customer's lounge as I performed what I thought would be a C-section. When I had Lulu fully opened, I observed a scene that appeared to be straight out of a horror show. The Uterus had ruptured and the pups had been released into the abdominal cavity. Fetal tissue is highly invasive so these pups had been absorbed into the liver, spleen, diaphragm and into the muscles of the abdominal wall. Parts of pups were sticking out of all of these organs. All of them were dead.

There was no way to save Lulu. I couldn't dissect the pups out of these tissues. They were too embedded and had compromised her blood flow and organ function. Lulu was dying.

I had to go to the lounge and talk to Joe. He wanted to see her before I euthanized her. I carried him back. He said his good byes and we let her go in peace.

Unfortunately, I didn't take pictures. Over my many years of practice, I never encountered an event like this and never talked with a vet who had seen a similar occurrence.

196

Twins?

I fancied myself as an expert at delivering calves. I had seen just about everything I thought.

I was called out to Jeremy's Dairy to assist a cow in labor. Jeremy had the cow in a chute with her head caught. I put on my shoulder length gloves and approached the cow from the rear. I lifted her tail and reached into her vagina.

I felt the head of a calf. It wasn't very large so I was surprised that she was having difficulty delivering. The calf was already dead so my main concern was delivering it without any damage to the cow.

When I applied a little pressure to extract the calf, it wouldn't budge. I reached in deeper and felt another calf.

"Ahhh"! I thought, "She has twins and they are tangled up".

I pushed and pulled and reached extremely deep into this cow and finally realized the twins weren't tangled they were joined. This was a case of conjoined twins.

The calves were separate from the head to the chest. There, they were joined down to the pelvis and the calves split again. The calves had two heads, two necks, and four front legs. They each had part of a chest and then the chest joined. They shared the abdomen and then split again at the hips. There were four back legs.

I couldn't tell all of this by palpation. I discovered this once I had removed everything. Once I realized what I was dealing with, I had a decision to make. Do I cut the calves in pieces and remove them vaginally or do I perform a C-Section and take them out of the cow's side?

Since the calves were already dead, I took the calves out in pieces to spare the cow major surgery.

Once I got all of the pieces out, we took lots of pictures. I carried the pictures to the newspaper but they wouldn't print them. They said it looked as if someone had cut up two calves and arranged them to look like conjoined twins.

I never had another pair.

Opps!

Harry had a heifer (a young cow that had never delivered a calf) that couldn't get up. She was out in his pasture and had been struggling a good part of the day. I went to his pasture and examined the heifer.

She was in labor but couldn't deliver her calf.

I put on my gloves and delivered the calf with ease. It weighed about 125lbs. This was a good size calf for a heifer. There was really no reason for her to be unable to rise.

Cows that produce large volumes of milk can get a condition called "milk fever". This occurs within the first three days after the cow has had a calf and is producing huge volumes of milk. Milk production uses the cows calcium and can draw the calcium to such a low level that the cows aren't able to stand. In rare cases the condition can occur before the cow calves and in even rarer conditions it will occur in heifers.

As I examined the heifer further, I reached back inside of her and low and behold, there was another calf. I delivered the second calf and to my surprise it was every bit as big as the first one.

I gave the heifer some calcium just to make sure I had covered everything. She was able to stand so I left the farm.

The very next mourning Harry called again. He had found the heifer down again and she wouldn't get up.

I returned to the farm and examined her again. Low and behold, there was a third calf in her. I delivered that one and the heifer was fine.

That was the only case of triplets in my days of practice.

So That's What It looks Like In A Cow

I was called one evening to a dairy farm. The owner said his cow was lying on her back and wouldn't get up.

I asked, "What do you mean, on her back?"

He said, "Exactly that, doc. She's on her back with her feet stuck straight up in the air."

I asked, "What happens when you roll her over?"

He said, "She goes right back on her back when we let go."

I had never heard such a thing. So I rushed to the farm. They led me to the cow and there she was, on her back with her legs stuck straight up in the air. My mouth dropped open. A cow would die if left in this position for too long.

Cow's have four compartments to their stomach and have to consistently belch to remove the tremendous amount of gases produced when they digest roughage (Grass, silage and hay) They need to be in an upright position to belch.

I rolled the cow over with the help of his herdsman and held her in place. No matter how long we held her, as soon as we let go she went right back on her back.

After trying everything, including trying to tie her in place, I tried sedation. I knocked her out for hours and waited to see what would happen. As soon as she woke up, back on her back she went.

I finally gave the dairyman a bottle anesthesia and told him to inject the cow every two hours through the night and we would see what occurred by morning.

I returned the next morning and rushed to find the cow. She wasn't where I had left her the day before. Encouraged I found the dairyman and inquired about the cow.

He answered, " She died," and he walked away.

I felt terrible. Not only had I lost the cow but I had no idea what was going on with this cow.

I walked slowly back to my truck and one of the hired hands called out to me, "Doc! You want to know what was wrong with that cow?"

"Sure!" I answered, "Do you have any ideas?"

He answered with certainty, "I know what happened to her."

I was intrigued. With all of my education and experience, I had no idea. But I was intelligent enough to know I didn't know everything. So I listened.

He came up real close to me, looked around to make sure he wasn't being watched, and whispered, "She got in the old man's marijuana patch." Then he walked away.

Wow!" Now I know how a cow on crack acts.

More Drugs

The Boyds were in there mid to late thirties. They had their 3 ½ lb Yorkshire Terrier with them. His tongue was hanging out and he was shaking all over. It looked like a case of poisoning. I was even more convinced of this when they said their other terrier was doing the same thing but not as bad.

I asked, "Is it possible the dogs ate something or got into anything that might have caused this?"

They said, "No."

I asked, "Do you have any kind of medication that the dogs could have found?"

Again, "No."

I told them to go and get the other dog. I would start a generalized poison treatment on this one.

The temperature was high as expected from a convulsing dog. I ran blood work and everything was in normal range. I hooked up an IV drip and gave the dog fluids in an effort to dilute whatever poison might be in its system. I was convinced this was a poison of some kind.

When the second dog was brought in, it was now in as bad a shape as the first. I sent the dog to the treatment room to start an IV drip on the second dog.

I told the owners, "I need to know what the dogs have gotten into in order to save them. If I knew the cause, I could probably save them. Not knowing, I was treating them generically."

The woman looked anxious and kept cutting her eyes to her husband. I could tell by her actions that she knew something and wanted to tell me, but her husband kept saying he knew nothing.

In exasperation, I said. "OK, I'll do the best I can. They will have to stay over night and I'll call you later to let you know how they are doing."

As they walked to the door and opened it, I tried one more time, "Knowing what I'm dealing with could be the difference between your dogs living or dying."

The woman turned around and looked straight at me and said, "My daughter had a party last night and some pretty rough looking guys were present. This morning when I went into the kitchen, I stepped on something that crunched under my foot. It was a brown, powdery substance".

I said, "Crack cocaine! Thank you."

I went to my office and quickly read how to treat a dog that had ingested cocaine. I treated the dogs and stayed with them late into the night.

They recovered completely.

When the Boyds came to the clinic to get their dogs, The husband said, "We went home and took another look at that powder and it turned out to be brown sugar'."

I smiled and said, "Yea! We treat brown sugar overdoses the same way we treat cocaine overdoses. Your dogs are fine."

Witches" Did IT

I read an article in the newspaper about a male horse in a local stable who had been mutilated by having his male organ cut off. The horse was still alive though he had lost a tremendous amount of blood. The horse had been in a locked stall. The stall door and the stall walls reached to the ceiling.

As days went by, there was more speculation about this case. Some thought a bikers' club was responsible. Others thought it was a "satanic ritual". I continued to stay out of the debate even though I had a fairly good idea of what had happened.

Another veterinarian had treated the horse and he thought someone with surgical skills had cut the horse's organ off.

A reward was offered for anyone who could identify the person(s) responsible.

Some people had seen lights deep into the night up in the hills of a nearby mountain. These were probably bootleggers. They have been known to shoot if anyone approached their stills.

The detective in charge of the case listed his number at the bottom of the article and requested he be called if anyone had any information.

I finally called him. I identified myself and explained that I had not seen the horse but was pretty sure I knew what happened. I told him male horses masturbate. Even geldings (castrated males) will do this. They get an erection and slam their organs (which are blood filled) against the underside of their abdomens with tremendous force.

I have treated two horses that had done this until the organ exploded like a blood filled balloon. One of the horses lived and the other died.

I reminded the detective that the horse's stall was still locked. There was no sign of the organ but a tremendous amount of blood in the stall.

I told him he could get ten of the biggest, strongest men he could find and put them in the stall with a horse and tell them to cut the horse's organ off. I promise him that some of those men will be seriously hurt if not killed. There was no sign of a struggle in the stall.

The detective was convinced that I knew what I was talking about. I told him to tell the owner and let the story fade from the newspaper.

I didn't want the veterinarian embarrassed. The detective closed the case and no more was written about it.

Third Child, Karen

Karen was born in July, three years after our last son. As she grew older, I could tell she had a real interest in animals. All of my kids liked to go on after hour calls especially if it involved delivering babies. I carried them as long as I knew it didn't interfere with school, homework or bedtime.

Karen was the only one of the three kids that may have become a veterinarian. Bryan couldn't stand the site of blood, Kevin wanted to be a doctor but for humans. Karen loved animals as much as I did.

When I carried the three of them to my clinic at night to watch a caesarean section on a cat or a dog, Karen and Kevin would race to the surgery room to claim one of the two stools in surgery so they could watch the procedure.

Bryan stayed outside of the surgery room. He never liked seeing blood.

Sometimes Karen would lean over the opened animal to the point I would have to say, "Karen, I appreciate your interest and I'm happy you want to get a good look, but I think it's more important that I get to see."

Karen would smile and move back a little.

One day Karen and I were alone in my truck, heading home from a calf delivery and I was talking to her. I said, "Karen, of all of the things that I do, bringing a life into the world and knowing I am responsible for it gives me a feeling of satisfaction that is immeasurable."

I paused for a moment and then said, "Can you imagine the feeling if that had been a human?"

206

It appeared as a light went off in Karen's head and that light never left. She is now an OBGYN in Atlanta, Georgia.

Kevin is also a medical doctor. He is a Physiatrist (physical medicine and rehabilitation) in Tampa, Florida.

Bryan works for Stabilis in Dallas, NC, managing some huge machine, the size of a small house. He has been with the company more than twenty years.

We are very proud of all of our children and each is special in their own way.

In Conclusion

If I could live my life over, I would probably change many things. There are two things I would never change. I would choose the same career and marry the same woman.

Not too many people can say that.

40258826R00122

Made in the USA
Charleston, SC
31 March 2015